"After reading the prologue and introduction I was hooked. Randy Long brings over 30 years of successful exit planning to help us all 'finish well.' You will be challenged to focus and even double down on your own family legacy planning; as Randy makes clear, many family businesses start well, but too few end well. You can be the exception with the BraveHeart Planning Process."

— **J. Keet Lewis**, Lewis Group International

"I highly commend Randy Long for his insight, wit and wise counsel. Randy is a trusted adviser and strategic thinker. After years of developing your business, I strongly recommend paying attention to Randy and his work."

— **Ted Baehr**, Founder, Christian Film & Television Commission Publisher and Editor-in-Chief of Movieguide® & Report to the Entertainment Industry

"*The BraveHeart Exit* is a powerful work with important instruction written by a true expert. Moving moments of history are woven into a very readable how-to manual regarding the best way to preserve wealth and, more importantly, legacy. I recommend this book to every business owner and anyone who aspires to build true wealth and share it with generations."

— **Kevin D. Freeman**, CFA, NY Times Best-Selling Author, Founder, NSIC Institute

"Filled with passion and conviction, Randy Long has written an important and insightful book that will help you be a better business owner, leader, and even parent."

— **Marcia Wieder**, Author, *DREAM*, CEO and Founder, Dream University

"Randy understands firsthand that entrepreneurship is the ultimate expression of personal freedom. With *The BraveHeart Exit*, Randy lays out the plan for us to carry this freedom into retirement while building a legacy. This book reminds us why we became entrepreneurs in the first place."

— **Mark Young**, CEO, Jekyll & Hyde Advertising

"You worked hard to grow your business. How can you ensure that your business continues to thrive when you move to the next phase of your life? Randy Long shares his best practices developed from over 30 years of successful exit planning to help you develop an optimal transition plan so you can leave the legacy you desire and deserve."

— **Elizabeth Lombardo**, PhD, Wealth Psychologist

"This is a brilliant book for owners of small-to-mid-sized businesses for several important reasons. First, 85 percent of owners fail to plan their exit. They are ultimately forced to close their doors instead of selling their businesses or passing them down to their families so their legacies live on. Second, owners looking to create a plan may have no idea where to start. Randy solves that problem with his 7-step process that is both practical and tactical. Finally, Randy provides business owners with a guide to follow in order to create a realistic valuation for their business. In short ... his book is a must-read."

— **Stephen Woessner**, Host of the top-rated Onward Nation podcast for business owners

"*The BraveHeart Exit* is a thorough, detailed, but eminently readable narrative about preparing and executing a successful transition for your business. Liberally sprinkled with stories from history, real client situations and his own experience, Randy wraps the lessons in entertainment and with writing that pulls you along happily from step to step. Anyone who is considering an eventual exit from his or her business should begin their research with *The BraveHeart Exit*."

— **John F. Dini**, Award-Winning Author, *Hunting in a Farmer's World*

THE BRAVEHEART EXIT

THE BRAVEHEART EXIT

7 Steps to Your Family Business Legacy

RANDY M. LONG

NEXT CENTURY
PUBLISHING

The BraveHeart Exit
7 Steps to Your Family Business Legacy

Published by Next Century Publishing
Las Vegas, Nevada
www.NextCenturyPublishing.com

ISBN: 978-1-68102-117-1
Library of Congress Control Number: 2015960284

Printed in the United States of America

*"Why are you planting those oak trees, Daddy?
You won't be around to enjoy them."*

*"See those large oak trees over there, Albert?
Someone planted those for us to enjoy!"*

-Albert Corbett, Family Business Owner

TABLE OF CONTENTS

THE BRAVEHEART EXIT

ACKNOWLEDGEMENTS

As my brother, David, was completing his book, he invited his publisher, Ken Dunn, over to meet me in hopes of convincing me to write a book. After a lengthy discussion about the kind of work my team and I do for business owners, Ken declared, "I think this would make an awesome book!" To which I replied, "Of course you do! Publishers think anything would make an awesome book." We laughed and here I am. So Ken, thanks for your persistence … you deserve the last laugh.

The bulk of my thanks, however, must go to my son, Micah and my daughter Ellen. I couldn't have completed this book without them.

Micah took a year off between his college graduation and the beginning of Law School at Liberty University to bring this project to life. His discipline was inspirational. Though he is not a content expert on the subject matter, he brought potentially dry material to life by the use of stories from history, politics and war. Almost every day, he would interview me on a particular subject and then write a rough draft of what we talked about. From there I would edit and he would edit and I would edit, and round we would go.

When we wanted another set of eyes on the material, we would bring in my daughters Ellen and Elisabeth, and my wife Lydia, for their input on the edits. Ellen, who was in the office every day with us, was constantly challenging us on the clarity of the writing and Lydia was relentless in her edits right up until the last day before printing. But hands down, Micah is the one that has invested the most time, energy and dedication. In fact, in that year, he did the rough draft of three books for our firm!

Ellen, drove also the messaging behind The BraveHeart Planning Process™. That development was not an easy task. Her love of business and her ability to clearly articulate concepts and processes were instrumental in building the foundation of the book and communicating what we do. So many thanks to Micah and Ellen for their hard work. I am very proud of both of you!

To my loyal office family, Jason, JoAnn, Herb, and Cheryl, thank you for keeping the businesses running. Your loyalty, dedication, and friendship over all these years mean the world to me.

To Matthew and Jonathan, I love you and am proud of who you are and what you have accomplished. I acknowledge that you are a big part of the inspiration behind the motivation to do the book. All in all, this has been a family project, which is why it is so special to me. Thank you all so much!

Author Randy M. Long with son Micah Long

FOREWORD

Having written several books about exit planning for business owners and read almost all others available, I can assure you this book will not disappoint. *The BraveHeart Exit* is one that only a battle-scarred attorney, wealth manager and certified exit planner could have written.

Unlike many authors in this crowded marketplace, Randy M. Long has fought the good fight of exit planning with many, many business owners. He has provided the tools and strategy needed to achieve their financial goals and aspirations as they exited their businesses. But Randy also understands owners in a way that many wealth managers do not. He realizes that maximizing our financial reward upon retirement is no small matter; yet this rarely motivates us to step away from what we love doing, nor does it give us the greatest satisfaction.

With that understanding and extensive experience as a foundation, Randy concentrates on creating an exit strategy that satisfies the same deeply-held convictions that first motivated us to go into business. He knows that we measure the benefits we receive by the benefits that we give to our families, and to those who remain in our companies, while we are at the helm and after we leave.

Don't get me wrong: maximizing our financial return is a fundamental requirement of a successful business exit. Yet, if our businesses are transferable at a price that yields us financial security, we are assured of making a good living. We don't have to sell to maintain our lifestyles.

We do, however, want to cut our exit plans from the same cloth we used to grow and run our companies. In *The BraveHeart Exit*, Randy shows us how to do exactly that. He shares how to use the exit planning process to create enduring legacies of family harmony and business culture that we have worked lifetimes to build.

If it isn't obvious at this point, I am a business owner. My company, Business Enterprise Institute, trains professionals like Randy in a seven-step exit planning process that thousands of owners have used. In *The BraveHeart Exit*, you'll get the best of both worlds: a tested, proven exit process and guidance and insight that only Randy can give. With Randy at your side, your exit strategy will give you the satisfaction—both financial and personal—that your business has given you for years.

John H. Brown, CEO, Business Enterprise Institute, Inc.

Author of three books:

The Completely Revised How To Run Your Business So You Can Leave It In Style
Cash Out Move On: Get Top Dollar—And More—Selling Your Business
Exit Planning—The Definitive Guide: Sell Your Business When You Want,
For the Money You Need, To the Person You Choose.

PREFACE

In the early years of my company, I remember reading a rather unsettling article in Inc. Magazine about an entrepreneur whose company was previously valued at $44 million dollars—only to see its market value eventually sink to zero. I remember thinking, *Well, that was a really stupid thing to allow to happen. Once his business started to decline, why didn't he do something, or at the very least seek wise counsel to help stop the bleeding before every cent he had invested was wiped out?* Sadly, the owner had to get a job working for someone else. I've never forgotten that story and have shared it with my team and many business friends through the years.

This story of business failure illustrates one of the many issues business owners face in building/protecting their enterprise when tough times arrive. However, there is another side that business owners must consider: What does the owner do when their business becomes successful? The choices are innumerable, and unless you have training in multiple areas of law, finance, tax, wealth management, exit planning, risk management, accounting expertise, and more, you would be wise to seek out those who do.

To be completely honest, I haven't always done that myself. Like many owners, I was focused on building my business and maintaining our annual growth goal of 20 percent increases every year. We accomplished this even in the tough years after 2008 when we increased our sales by 35 percent in 2009 and 41 percent in 2010. Being distracted by our success, I didn't realize how much damage I was doing by *not* incorporating wealth management/exit planning/estate and tax planning strategies. I didn't think I was "making enough money to worry about it yet." I was wrong, and it cost me big time!

If I could go back in time, I would have sought the wisdom of experts who could have helped me plan and protect the success of my business and the lives of our fifty-six employees.

Enter Randy M. Long, my brother, the expert.

Okay, a confession from me. The Bible says, "A prophet is without honor in his own country." Yes, I completely ignored the fact that Randy is a nationally recognized expert in helping business owners and entrepreneurs set up their lives to maximize their business success. I didn't take his advice seriously when he first said we needed to sit down and plan out the next few years. He was trying to help me protect my business, my family, and my team. I thought, *Man, we're rocking it and making more profit than ever before! Meeting with Randy can wait a little longer!* And "wait" I did—regrettably.

When I finally had enough sense to listen to Randy and sit down with him and his team to analyze "where we were and where we wanted to be," he showed me how I had already paid way too much money in taxes, and had put my business and employees in danger by not adequately creating a successful strategy in advance.

I prefer not to disclose the amount of money I wasted. I will, however, be happy to tell you how Randy eventually helped me create a strategy for my business entities that transferred some of the company assets into a trust for our children before we grew the business any larger. This move alone has saved my sweet wife, Janet, and me millions in death/inheritance taxes as our business has continued to grow (up 29 percent YTD). It also protects my children and grandchildren for generations to come.

As they say, "Hindsight is 20/20." With that in mind, here is the cold, hard truth I will always have in the back of my mind: "IF I had been intelligent enough to meet with Randy and his team earlier when he asked me to, I would have saved myself seven figures, conservatively, in wasted resources. I can't get that money back! It's gone. Man that hurts just saying it! I sincerely wish I had acted sooner.

Now it's your turn to decide. Will you listen, or will you ignore sound wisdom? What you're about to learn from reading Randy's book will radically change your life and greatly enhance the success of your business for years to come. After realizing the mistakes I had made (and the money I wasted), I insisted he write this book to help educate other arrogant, know-it-all, you-can't-tell-me-anything business owners like myself who aren't fortunate to have Randy as their brother. You're welcome. ☺

Thank you, Randy, for pestering me until I listened.

Your truly grateful brother,

David Long, CEO

MyEmployees www.MyEmployees.com

Author, *Built to Lead*

Wilmington, NC

910-392-9663

Pieux quoique preux

Long

PROLOGUE

I come from a family of lions. It is fitting that the Long family crest has a lion standing tall on his back legs ready for battle, with the family motto written above: *"Pieux Quoique Preux"*—Devout though Valiant. This motto is the underlying theme that connects the men of my family, past and present.

My ancestors came to America from the British Isles early in this country's history. They were some of the first pioneers to settle in southeastern North Carolina. As far back as we know, the men in my family were strong and tough. They were brawlers—fiercely independent and self-employed—or they were pastors. It was into this confusing mix of independence, faith, and fists that I was born. I was raised hearing stories of these men.

Family legend has it that my granddaddy Jesse went to the World's Fair in the 1930s and knocked out the world champion boxer. Seems the champion was offering anyone in the crowd the chance to go a few rounds with him. My grandpa Jesse stepped up to the challenge and knocked him out in the second round. Grandpa Jesse loved his family of six children dearly, but he battled all his life with alcoholism. My dad was the oldest, which often put him in the crosshairs of his father when he was drunk. Though my dad had all the other male family traits, he never touched a drop of alcohol. When he was young, he overheard his mother praying in her room that he would never drink. Seeing the effect his father's drinking had on his mother made a profound impact on him. By the grace of God, my siblings and I were not raised with an alcoholic father but by one who pursued his passion to know and serve the Lord.

I am the second of six children: five boys and one girl. Since my dad pastored small country churches, we grew up with little in the way of material things. We were a close-knit family, loved by both parents but largely held together by my mother, who ran the world for us. My mother always told me when I was growing up that I could be anything I imagined. Dad taught us the Scriptures, the difference between right and wrong, and how to defend ourselves. If you went out for a sport, you played to the end of the season, no exceptions. You counted the cost of anything that you decided to do, because you would be doing it for a very long time.

> **My mother always told me growing up I could be anything I imagined**

Small business is also in my blood. I've been working in it my entire life. I learned a great deal from working for small business owners during my youth. I also had a few business ventures of my own from high school through college—things like mowing grass and painting houses. In college, I had the brilliant idea to sell two-day-old bakery goods to the other athletes in their dorms at night. As with many entrepreneurs, I was doing quite well until I was shut down by regulation; it seems the college did not want competition on campus for their vending machines!

While in college, I obtained a half-scholarship in track, which is an amazing story of God's provision in my life. The scholarship, along with many long nights of work at a variety of jobs, helped me graduate with no debt. I majored in business, with an emphasis on personal finance. I was intrigued by the personal finance industry and knew I wanted to know how to make money, since I was no fan of poverty. I was all about starting a small business of my own.

Upon graduation in 1982, I headed for California to pursue my girl. When I arrived in Los Angeles, my dear great aunt agreed to let me live with her indefinitely, until I could get on my feet.

My evenings and weekends were spent working to obtain my Series 7 stock brokerage securities license. Once I had that license, I put on my blue suit and went down to the Newport Beach office of the first Wall

Street brokerage firm I could find. I made an appointment with the branch manager and I explained to him the work I wanted to do. As I talked, he picked up a piece of paper sitting in the middle of his desk and kept looking at it. I thought he wasn't paying attention.

I pressed on anyway. After about fifteen minutes of talking, he stopped me and said, "I was given direction from the New York office two weeks ago to fill a position exactly like you described."

He ran his hand through his hair. "It's incredible! I didn't know how I was ever going to find someone in time." He then reached across the desk and handed me the piece of paper. "I guess this is meant for you. The job is yours if you can be in New York in six weeks." While I was with the brokerage firm, I obtained my CFP® (Certified Financial Planner) designation through the University of Southern California.

After a few years, I sensed a disconnection between what clients needed and how the professional world segmented advice, instead of coordinating and collaborating together for the benefit of the client. So, I decided to go to law school to learn more about serving family businesses.

For many years, I ran two separate businesses in California, which were located side by side: a legal practice that focused on estate planning and business organizations and a wealth management firm that focused on building and preserving family legacies.

In 2007, we moved to North Carolina to be with my extended family. Several years later, I added the Certified Exit Planning (CExP) designation to my credentials and we opened a Wilmington, North Carolina office. Today, I get to work with and teach my children the practice of wealth management, business consulting, and what we call BraveHeart Planning™, the subject of this book.

For more than thirty years, I have represented, counseled, and advised hundreds of family business owners to plan for the transition of their companies to the next generation or to prepare their companies for sale. I believe there will be more demand for exit planning—including our BraveHeart Planning™—than there are qualified advisors. Why?

Because, more businesses will transition in the next ten years than at any other time in history, due to the retirement of the Baby Boomer generation. Supply and demand will come into play, making it harder to sell than you probably expect. The companies that are run in such a way that makes them more valuable to buyers will sell, and for better prices than their competitors. A great deal of money can be made or lost depending on whether this is done well.

> **More businesses will transition in the next ten years than at any other time in history.**

I wrote this book to provide a basic roadmap for you, the business owner. This book will teach you to plan for the transition of the business to your family, or to sell to the buyer you want, at the time you want, for the price you want. Since you cannot choose how long you will live or whether you will stay healthy, your business needs to be continuously prepared for a transition. You will also learn how to put the business in tip-top shape so that it can transition successfully under any set of circumstances.

Families fail because they lose sight of what is important. Leo Tolstoy once wrote, "All happy families are alike; each unhappy family is unhappy in its own way." Happy families are alike because the principles that create happy families are timeless; they transcend culture, location, and the laws of man. There are thousands of ways to ruin the happiness of a family, just as there are thousands of ways to fail in business. As a family grows in wealth and size, the ways to fail grow exponentially. But only by sticking to the timeless principles of love and trust, honor and forgiveness, can a family hold on to its legacy.

I also wrote this book because I want to help America. I believe it is more vital than ever that our nation encourages these businesses with fewer regulations and lower taxes. We now live in a globally competitive environment. We can compete with the world and win if our government, and its hell-bent desire for regulation and control, will get out of the way.

America is spending not just our children's money with our extreme national debt but also our grandchildren's. In the following pages, I hope to encourage us all to build strong families, families that leave a legacy of lasting values and commitment to each other and to our country.

Finally, I wrote this book because becoming a Legacy Family is a journey my family is on. It is a journey full of challenges, hard work, and faith. It is my goal to live and leave my own legacy. And, on the way, I want to challenge you to live and leave a legacy of family, faith, and fortune of your own.

Please understand that even as I hope to challenge you, I am not holding out my family or myself as a perfect example. We have failed each other and have made mistakes that have left scars. We still have to repent, forgive, and love by the grace of God. We are learning as we grow, and we want you on this journey with us.

I have a love for history. Because it is important to learn from the past, each of the following chapters will depict a scene from history during a time of challenge and duress. Each will have a lesson that can be learned and applied to our BraveHeart Planning Process™. When you understand the story behind the battles, it is all about planning, logistics, and execution. You, as a business owner, will need all of those as you work through your own successful BraveHeart Planning Process™.

The stories and examples used in this book are compilations of persons and situations over many years. Names, places, dates and pertinent details have all been altered. A resemblance to any situation or person, living or dead, is purely coincidental.

INTRODUCTION:

Everything Rises and Falls on Leadership

This book is primarily written for those who have a business that is—or can be made into—more than just a job for the owner. This is not a textbook, nor is it an exhaustive treatment of any particular subject. This book gives the small to mid-sized business owner a roadmap to creating a BraveHeart Plan that will allow him to live a legacy as well as leave one. BraveHeart Planning™ takes a leader that is willing to make the hard choices, for both family and business. That leader is you.

> **BraveHeart Planning takes a leader who is willing to make the hard choices.**

Independence, faith, and freedom are the bedrock upon which America was founded. Her people came seeking freedom of religion, freedom from tyranny, and the opportunity for financial independence. America's first families used those advantages to create hundreds of thousands of small businesses, which grew her into the greatest power the world has ever seen. Nowhere else in the world could the average man become his own master by his hard work and quick wit. They called it *the American dream.*

That dream originated from those who lived under oppression. Part of my background includes the Scots-Irish, a people whose history is filled with stories of independence and strength. The Highland Scots were one of the few populations who stopped the Roman Empire. The entire Ninth Legion, 6000 soldiers strong, reportedly vanished into the soggy moors of Northern Scotland, succumbing to the guerilla tactics of wild Celtic warriors. Unable to advance further, the Romans built Hadrian's

Wall to shut the Scots out. Today, it still stands as a memorial to their invincible spirit.

That spirit lived on in 1297, when William Wallace defeated a vastly larger army of English noblemen at the Battle of Stirling Bridge. Former Virginia Senator James Webb, chronicler of the Scots-Irish legacy, gives an assessment of Wallace's character that I couldn't agree with more:

> Here, in contrast to the calculating royal class, was a leader who fought not for fame or reward, but in pursuit of his nation's honor. Here was a man who had persisted despite the betrayal of the self-seeking higher nobility that always had seemed more concerned about their titles and their lands than their nation. And here was a national martyr who, with his last words in the face of a certain and horrible death, spoke only about the justness of his people's cause.[1]

William Wallace exemplified leadership in a way unmatched by the Scottish Lords who were both richer and better educated, not to mention blessed with positions of leadership. William Wallace led, not by lording it over his followers, but by laying down his life to serve his country.

William Wallace and his denial of self-interest is a role model, not just for military commanders, but leaders of all organizations, especially family businesses. We are going to spend the book walking through the strategies and tactics a family business can employ to strengthen, revitalize, and transition the business. But all my words will be wasted if the family members that own the business cannot learn to put the needs of the family before their own. It is far better to have a healthy family and a broken business than the other way around.

I love working with family businesses. This allows business to be used in such a way that it creates stronger families. In my opinion, family business matters because family matters. But even if you don't agree with me, you must admit that family businesses have a huge impact on the U.S. economy. According to a study conducted by noted researchers Joseph H. Astrachan and Melissa Carey Shanker, family businesses account for 50 percent of U.S. gross domestic product, generate 60 percent of the country's employment, and account for 78 percent of all new job creation.[2] But when was the last time you heard politicians promote family businesses or make it easier for those businesses to thrive?

In the last fifty years, the importance of family business, at least in the minds of politicians and the public, has fallen precipitously by the wayside and so have their numbers. As a result, family businesses are increasingly in danger. They are faltering as a direct result of the breakdown of the nuclear family and ever-growing governmental regulation and taxation.

Family businesses fight to succeed on two fronts. On one front, they face relational and societal challenges. On the other they face increased regulation, rising healthcare costs, and increased competition from international players. As a result, for the first time in thirty-five years, more businesses are dying than are being born.[3] Additionally, the government has not been kind to family businesses. Regulation is squeezing margins, and government debt has increased the economy's risk and volatility by exponential factors.

We also see the trend toward big government begetting big business and vice versa. Each protects and feeds on the other in a symbiotic relationship. Big business finances the elections and pressures Congress with their expensive lobbyists. The politicians then provide tax breaks, tax credits, and political pork to those big businesses. They pass legislation and regulations that require the hiring of lawyers and accountants to comply. This drives up the costs of business to the smaller businesses who cannot allocate it over millions of products sold. This protects profits for the big businesses even more. The big businesses may even get exemption from the regulations, like the corporate exemptions granted to those companies who do not want to be part of Obamacare. The big businesses then spend some of those profits on electing people and the cycle goes on and on, at the expense of the small to medium businesses and the individual taxpayer.

But one the most imposing challenges to family business is endurance. Countless numbers of family businesses have been unable to successfully transfer the business to the next generation. In fact, the landscape of history is littered with such businesses, all failing to manage their roles as owners and family members. Almost every culture has a saying that communicates this truth. The English version is "shirt-sleeves to shirt-sleeves in three generations." In China, this phenomenon is known as "rice paddy to rice paddy in three generations." My favorite rendition is the Arabic understanding of this phenomenon, which is both poetic and prophetic:

> The first generation retains the desert qualities, desert toughness, and desert savagery...they are brave and rapacious, greatly feared...the strength of group feeling continues to be preserved among them. Under the influence of royal authority and a life of ease, the second generation changes from the desert attitude to a sedentary culture, from privation to luxury and plenty, from a state in which everybody shared in the glory to one in which one man claims all the glory...others are [in]...humble subservience...the vigor of the group feeling is broken... But many of the old virtues remain...because they had direct personal contact with the first generation...The third generation, then, has (completely) forgotten the period of desert life and toughness...Luxury reaches its peak among them...Group feeling disappears completely... People forget to protect and defend themselves...In the course of these three generations, the dynasty wears away.[4]

The first generation works extremely hard to create and build the family business. The second generation sees the value of hard work, and benefits from it. But the third generation often squanders the wealth and destroys the business. The numbers are telling: only three percent of family businesses last more than two generations.[5]

Since family business is such an integral actor in the economy, it is important to know why family enterprises succeed and why they fail. With such a staggeringly bad track record, it is apparent that family businesses do not succeed on accident, they don't last by happenstance, and they most certainly do not achieve longevity by apathy. In order to leave a legacy, families have to work hard and must create a plan. The natural tendency of everything is entropy—to drift into oblivion. Left to themselves, relationships break down, quality drops, laziness sets in, and money is squandered.

The integration of all the factors of success, on both a personal and professional level, proves to be incredibly complex. Family relationships and business solutions must work in tandem for the family business to survive. It is at this nexus that we strive to strengthen the family through the business and the business through the family. If families are unable to successfully navigate the swirling waters ahead, the American economy will feel the impact.

I don't care what generation you happen to represent within your family business; you can be the leader your business and your family needs to successfully build and transition to the next generation.

Will you take on the challenge to lead your family and your business? Accepting that role will help you live your legacy. By living it now, you will also be able to leave one. You will need to love your family and your employees enough to spend money on growing and planning for the family and the business. You will need foresight and a willingness to implement your plan. You will need to consider their interests along with your own. You will need to be the kind of person that leads in such a way that he lives and leaves a legacy. It takes a lion. Stand up and roar!

CHAPTER 1

The Reason

Robert Johnson owned a successful architectural firm. He was a devoted husband and father to a beautiful family. He worked hard for many years and was finally reaping the fruits of his labor. Robert had his good days and bad days, but no matter what happened the day before, he woke up every morning feeling like he was on top of the world.

On April 13, 2004, tragedy struck Robert's family. That morning, Robert boarded his firm's private plane, intending to visit a client. But at approximately 8:30 a.m., the plane went down and he was killed. Only 51 years old, Robert Johnson breathed his last breath early that spring morning—and the future of his business and his family changed forever.

Like so many of us, Robert loved what he did and sincerely thought he would continue doing the same thing for the next twenty years. He never considered leaving his business, and he did not plan a thoughtful strategy to facilitate the transition.

The plane crash resulting in Robert's death was truly a tragedy, but the loss of a husband and father wasn't the only thing his family and community lost. Because Robert had never stepped back and asked himself, "What would happen to my family, my business, and my employees if I were not here tomorrow?" his wife Susan was forced to answer those questions on her own.

Robert alone held the architectural license for the firm in the three-state region where his firm worked. As a result, Susan had to close down the firm and lay off the firm's twenty-eight employees, leaving their families devastated and forcing them to look elsewhere for employment. She sold the firms' assets at fire sale prices, realizing very little from her husband's company. That wasn't the scenario Robert and Susan had expected to end his career. What went wrong?

Failing to plan is planning to fail. The tragic loss of Robert's business could have been avoided. I remember sitting down with him, begging him to get started on his planning. He just shook his head and said, "I'll get to it soon. I'm just not ready right now." Robert was unwilling to take the time and effort to make sure his family and his business were protected because he was "too busy."

As unfortunate as it is, stories like Robert's are not rare. Well-meaning, successful business people are forced out of their businesses everyday by events beyond their control. As a matter of fact, a 2010 study by PricewaterhouseCoopers found that 85 percent of business owners have no exit strategy and 65 percent have no idea what their business is worth; yet of those surveyed, 75 percent of their net worth was tied up in their businesses.[6]

On an emotional level, I understand why so few owners have a plan. Contemplating your exit forces you to confront your hopes, dreams, ambitions, relationships, struggles, and even your own mortality and physical fragility. At the end of the day, transitioning a business is a daunting proposition. However, on a cognitive and strategic level, having no exit plan makes little sense. Managing your transition—whether that is to the next generation of your family, to your employees, or to an outside buyer—is the most crucial portion of your family's financial well-being. The failure to plan for your transition is the greatest threat to your family business, bar none.

> **The failure to plan for your transition is the greatest threat to your family business.**

Planning your transition involves looking forward to your ideal outcome. However, it also involves contingency planning in case circumstances do not allow you to reach your goal in the way you had planned. It is a competitive world out there. Ideally, we like to have a client work with us five to ten years prior to a planned transition to get the family and the company ready.

If you are planning on selling to a third party, it won't be easy. Over the next few years, you will be only 1 of the 8 million business owners intent on selling their business.[7] Competition for buyers will be high. Prices may drop as these millions of businesses hit the market around the same time. It is a pure supply and demand problem: not enough buyers and too many sellers.

Though mergers and acquisitions (M&A) activity is at a historic high right now, this trend will inevitably abate because it is cyclical. When this uptrend has run its course, it will enter a downtrend that could last for a number of years. My personal assessment is that we probably have another two or three years left of strong M&A activity, given interest rates, available leverage, and dry powder (investible money still on the sidelines). In the coming market, firms could be sold at rock bottom prices, or not at all. Only businesses run in a world-class manner are likely to command a premium price for sale.

Do you have a plan to confront this tough market? Odds are you don't. Seven out of ten business owners have no exit plan of any kind. Worse than that, five out of ten family businesses have no buy/sell agreement, which means the very survival of their business is in danger.[8] Of those attempting to sell to third parties, the number one reason a transaction fails is a lack of preparation on a seller's part.[9] Unfortunately for the majority of business owners out there today, hope is not a winning strategy for your planning.

> **The number one reason a transaction fails is a lack of preparation on a seller's part.**

Like my friend Robert, one day you will exit your business—planned or unplanned! Getting your business sold may take less than a year, but as I mentioned, planning for the best outcome should begin five to ten years before your planned transition. Since none of us is guaranteed tomorrow, the sooner you start the better.

Whether you sell or transition, today's environment makes planning more critical than it has ever been. Nearly 50 percent of successful business owners plan on exiting their companies before 2020.[10]

Most of these companies will fail to achieve the objectives of their founders. Hundreds of thousands of businesses across the nation will see their chief executives and leaders retire or die with no plans for succession or with inadequate transition tactics that fail to produce results. Even firms that have plans in place will still falter due to poor implementation and mismanaged exit processes. They become stale over time.

But it doesn't have to be this way. A transition may be fraught with challenges, but it is also rich with opportunity. It provides family businesses the chance to make the most of their assets and preserve a lasting institution that reflects the family's ideals and goals long after the founders are gone. You must not fear a business exit; instead, see it as an opportunity to lay a foundation for a lasting legacy!

Legacy building must start today. It begins with the first decision and continues on into the hazy mist of the future, long after you are gone. It is meant to be enjoyed both now and later. A truly great legacy is one that stands the test of time. It is an ideal or a set of values that continues long after the founding father is laid to rest. True legacies are those internalized by the successor generation and acted upon year after year.

Several years ago, I had the pleasure of working with a client named Tom. Tom's dad had started a successful manufacturing company just before World War II. After returning home from the war, Tom joined the company. When his dad died in 1965, Tom took over. Tom was getting on in years and I understood that we would be approaching the higher end of the private equity purchase cycle before too long.

One day I approached him and asked, "Have you considered planning to prepare your business for sale?"

Tom replied, "Actually I have been thinking for the past few years about what I am going to do with my company since none of my kids have any interest in it."

Despite years of ruminating on it, Tom had never gotten around to actually creating a plan for his exit.

To accomplish Tom's business objectives, I created a plan that called for a sale to a third party that incorporated various family goals. I pulled a team together and began working to implement the plan. We (the team) introduced a number of ideas to reduce company risk and to increase the value of the company over the next two years.

Tom brought in a CEO in order to exhibit the fact that the business could operate without him. We also added stay bonuses for a few key employees to make sure that they would stay for a few years after the sale to transition the new ownership. Tom spent the final year before the sale working on the business instead of in it.

We also created a plan for the family that included how Tom wanted the funds distributed upon the sale. Tom had plans for what he wanted to do for the years following his retirement, including working on his ranch, traveling with his wife, and spending lots of time with his grandkids. He also wanted to eliminate estate taxes. All of his objectives for the family were realized because Tom was proactive about planning.

Tom had a sister with a minority ownership interest due to a gift from her dad. She lived well but had not put away necessary funds for her retirement. She did not work in the business, so without the sale, she would not have realized her share of the value in her lifetime. The sale of the company solved her liquidity issue and funded her retirement.

On the day of his exit, Tom sold his company for the amount he wanted, to the buyer he chose, and within his desired timeframe. Whether your company is worth $5 million or $50 million, Tom's story encapsulates a successful exit. The BraveHeart Planning Process™ increases value, both in the short-term and in the long-term. It is measurable, put in writing, and provides accountability in the form of deadlines for both the owner and his advisors.

Before you begin your own BraveHeart Planning Process™, you must first determine where you currently stand. The Business Enterprise Institute, located in Denver, Colorado, is where I received my exit planning certification. The institute provides a short quiz to help you assess where you are in the planning process for a transition. If you are like most business owners, you will find numerous areas that you have neglected.[11]

1. Do you know your primary planning objectives in leaving the business, such as departure date, desired price, and designated successor?

2. Do you know your income needed to achieve financial security?

3. Do you know how much your business is worth?

4. Do you know how to increase the value of your ownership interest through enhancing the most valuable asset of the company: the employees?

5. Do you know the best way to sell your business to a third party in order to maximize your cash, minimize your tax liability, and reduce your risk?

6. Do you know how to transfer your business to family members, co-owners, or employees while paying the least possible taxes and enjoying maximum financial security?

7. Have you implemented all necessary steps to insure that the business continues if you don't?

8. Have you provided for your family's security and continuity if you die or become incapacitated?

If you are like every business owner I have worked with, you will only be able to answer yes to a few of these questions. However, the continuity of your business and the security of your family depend on you being able to answer in the affirmative to each and every one of these questions. I have written this book and have dedicated my career to helping business owners like you to answer yes to those questions.

Too often, business owners approach their exit with a narrow perspective, focusing only on the business side and ignoring family legacy. They ignore the familial implications of selling or transferring their business. As a result, I have seen countless families suffer by adopting an ill-fated transition process—which is why I created my own process to operate at the intersection of business and family. I created the BraveHeart Planning Process™ to equip you to live your legacy, both today and every day of the rest of your life.

The BraveHeart Planning Process™

1. The Decision

2. The Resources

3. The Team

4. Value Catalysts

5. Business Durability

6. The Legacy Builder

7. Life after Transition

How It Works

The BraveHeart Planning Process™ takes a holistic approach to the future of your business and family. Instead of focusing solely on selling, the business owner and the planner work together to create a lasting legacy in the business and in the family, simultaneously. It isn't enough to exit with a wad of cash or leave the business to your children through inheritance. Your exit from the business should be used to strengthen your family not just obtain the highest price or see that the business stays in the family.

Exiting your business properly is a complicated process, but with the right team of advisors in place—acting in the owner's best interests—the solution is well within reach.

What does it mean to be prepared for an exit? To be successful, business owners need to have a realistic expectation of what the process will look like. The key is to take the process one step at a time. Following the BraveHeart Planning Process™ gives owners the power to take control of their final destination. You systematically work through my 7-step process that incorporates wealth management, business growth, and exit planning components.

Engaging in the BraveHeart Planning Process™ will help you:

- Define your unique goals and objectives

- Make sure your business will continue if something should happen to you before your planned exit

- Increase the value of your company so you reap maximum value for your life's work

- Create retirement and asset management strategies that give you the level of comfort and freedom you desire

- Strengthen your family

Exit plans are as unique as the owners who create them, yet all transitions flow through the same themes. The specifics are always different, but the general principles employed in the BraveHeart 7-step Planning Process hold true for all transitions.

Why Go Brave?

Go brave for freedom, flexibility, responsibility, and family. The BraveHeart Planning Process™ positions you to take advantage of all the best reasons you own a family business, and it helps you manage the risks associated with self-employment.

Freedom. Family business owners are united around a single passion: their love of freedom. I interviewed almost a hundred owners, and every single one told me the best thing about owning a business is the freedom it provides. The BraveHeart Planning Process™ was created to equip owners to realize/enjoy the freedoms of ownership, rather than becoming slaves to their businesses.

Flexibility. It is somewhat paradoxical that owners prize freedom so highly, because most of them have far less free time than their employees. The key difference, however, is control. Owners find freedom not in volume of time, but in choice. They love the ability to take the time when they choose. They work because they want to work, not because someone forces it upon them. For much of their business life, they have worked harder and longer than employees; they just want to do it on their own terms.

Responsibility. Business owners also love the personal accountability that comes with owning a business. When things go wrong, there is no one else to blame. They love living in the economy of results rather than the economy of effort. They want to be measured for their effectiveness, not on how long they've punched a clock. Some describe self-employment as "eating what you kill." It is graphic, but it makes the point. Every day is a hunt; every moment is a thrill. The wins are bigger, but so are the losses. Most people can't accept the responsibility, so most people do not own businesses.

> Entrepreneurs love living in the economy of results rather than the economy of effort.

Family. It is especially difficult to be faithful in your family roles when you own a business. The owner's work is never done and it is a challenge to know when to quit for the day and be present with the family when you go home. Those relationships need to be grown and protected. The balance is not easy. Not everyone can successfully juggle business and family, which is why most fail.

Being self-employed can be fun and incredibly satisfying, but it also brings never-ending challenges and loads of stress. Add to that the dynamic of employees and family and things only compound. It's obvious that leading a successful family business is not for the faint of heart!

So, why go brave? Because the BraveHeart Planning Process™ not only helps you preserve your freedom, your choices, your responsibility, and your family relationships, it serves as a guide for doing each of them well. It also provides a roadmap to help you increase your free time, grow your business, increase its durability, and provide you with the resources to fund every stage of your life and maybe even generations to come.

> Every day is a hunt; every moment is a thrill.

Will you join me on my quest to live and leave a legacy that celebrates entrepreneurism, family, and faith? The challenge is to become a leader that builds a legacy of financial and relational strength and wisdom at work and at home—a BraveHeart.

The BraveHeart Vision

BraveHeart is a code.

Having a BraveHeart doesn't mean you paint your face, strap on a sword and go charging around the neighborhood yelling "Freedom!" But it does mean you have a heart set on fire with passion. It is a fire that demands excellence and loves a challenge.

BraveHeart is a code that holds to the fact that there is more to life than making money and providing for one's offspring is more than just giving them money and a place to live. It means teaching them, equipping them, and giving them space to grow in areas that are not taught in our education system. BraveHeart is a pride in quality, in a job well done, in your family, your business, and the work of your hands. It is the desire to be a steward in every area of your life.

> **Running a family business isn't for the faint of heart; it takes a BraveHeart**

BraveHeart is the code that applies an attitude of resolution in the face of opposition. It is a state of quiet strength in spite of hostility. It is a way of living that looks at the challenges of life and says, "No more!" No more will I blame others for my pain, no more will I shirk my responsibility for my actions, and no more will I refuse to act because I am afraid of failing.

BraveHeart is the code that caused the Pilgrims to risk a perilous ocean crossing for religious freedom, and it is the code that compelled millions of immigrants to seek a new life in America. It is the same code by which the servicemen and women of our country live, the same code by which they die.

The BraveHeart code isn't just about doing extraordinary deeds. It calls up the courage to face the humdrum of an ordinary life without complaint. It demands devotion to duty in the face of boredom and broken dreams. It holds that one's actions matter, that God sees the small things.

Adherents to the code choose to do what is right, whether or not someone is watching, whether or not it is popular or profitable. They don't settle for less than they can or less than they can be. They accept duty and responsibility. You won't find BraveHearts walking out on their families. They make mistakes, but they never give up. They ask for forgiveness and give it, even when they don't feel like it. BraveHearts love others more than they love themselves. They are givers, not takers. They love their families, their businesses, and their countries.

A code is never real until it is acted upon. To claim the BraveHeart code, you cannot simply have a brave heart, you must be a BraveHeart. It's a way

> ## Bravehearts are not born; they are forged.

of life, a state of being. If you have not applied yourself as you should, you must resolve to clean up your messes and live a responsible life. You begin to dream again and work toward those dreams, because your future is largely dependent on you and your attitudes and efforts.

BraveHeart is a process.

BraveHearts are not born; they are forged. They are fashioned in the crucible of adversity; they are hammered out on the anvil of hard work; they are sharpened on the unforgiving edge of ownership; and they are refined on the grinder of familial responsibility. They rise to the task that is set before them.

A BraveHeart doesn't just wake up one morning and see a hero in the mirror. Becoming a BraveHeart isn't a transformation; it is a journey of heartache, sweat, tears, and triumphs.

The process involves preparation. A BraveHeart plans ahead, not waiting for disaster to strike his family, the economy to hit his business, or laziness and infighting to take hold. A BraveHeart sees what comes ahead and acts accordingly, to the best of his or her ability.

Becoming a BraveHeart is a formidable undertaking. That is why I built this process: to help true BraveHearts develop a roadmap for their business and family as they plan and work for today and the future. Those who go through the BraveHeart Planning Process™ will have their passions and hard work directed to channels that they may not currently see in order to meet goals and challenges for which they are not yet ready.

BraveHeart is a movement.

The family unit is under challenge and stress. Though this is surely a business book, it is one that highlights the importance of cherishing your family and leading it—along with your business—and having each positively impact the other. Together, your family and business will also positively impact our country.

> Ours is not a fight of bullets or swords, but it is a fight nonetheless.

The reason for going through the BraveHeart Planning Process™ is not just to get a great price for your business or make sure that your retirement is secure, but to help you strengthen your family now and in the future. I want you to live your legacy as well as leave one. Together, we will discover what that means to you. But whatever it is, I know it includes growing your family relationships, as well as being successful in business.

BraveHeart is the code, the process, and the movement that creates BraveHearts. But each are worthless without execution. It is not enough to simply start. You have to follow through and finish.

I wrote this book because I believe in this country and the families who run its core businesses. The reason my family crest is included on page 18 is because I'm proud of my family. I'm proud of where I've come from and I'm excited about where my family is heading. The fight for family is not a fight of bullets or swords today, but it is a fight nonetheless. As a BraveHeart business owner, you must work hard to successfully grow and transition your business. You must work hard to invest your time and energy into loving and shepherding your family, and you must invest in yourself to become the person you were meant to be.

CHAPTER 2

The Decision

Philadelphia, July 4, 1776

The hot air blew through the opened windows. Fifty-six men sat around a long table, sweat dripping off their powdered wigs in the baking July heat. A sacred hush seemed to envelope the room as the men pondered the impact of their decision. The time had come; their lives, their fortunes, and their sacred honor were at stake. Nine would pay the ultimate sacrifice for their names quilled on that brown parchment paper. Seventeen would lose their land, places they fought so bravely to save, and leave every last penny behind. Some would count the cost, and refuse to pay the price. After the bloodshed that later ensued, John Adams would later write he would have given anything to have returned to the way things were before that fateful day.

Something had to be done, though. The events leading up to the signing of the Declaration of Independence had precipitated a necessary response. The Boston Massacre was still fresh on the fledging nation's mind. Months earlier, Patrick Henry had aroused the people's spirit with his fiery proclamation, "Give me liberty, or give me death." The British had spoken. The midnight ride of Paul Revere and William Dawes had barely saved the nascent army from utter annihilation. The clash at Lexington and Concord became the "shot heard 'round the world." And George Washington had stepped up to take the helm as commander-in-chief of the Continental Army a mere two months before. Up until now, however, it was merely the uprising of a rebel colony. The Declaration would change everything.

The men huddled around the table knew the effect this document could have. Britain's wrath would soon be unleashed, and full-scale war would quickly be upon them. Signing it would change not only their lives, but also the lives of their countrymen everywhere.

But one man did not hesitate. With large, swooping swirls, he stepped up first and inscribed his name on a document that would turn the world upside down. With fire in his eyes, John Hancock stepped up to that table and boldly declared, "There! King George can read that without spectacles; let the British ministry double their reward."

Men like John Hancock make a decision and never look back. John Hancock knew what he was getting into. He knew the danger and he knew the risk, but he pressed on anyway because he believed that freedom was more important than life itself. While very few business owners must put their lives on the line, every single one of them faces a decision: "Will I prepare my family and business for my exit, or will I leave it to the winds of fortune to decide?" The stakes may not be life and death, but they are high nonetheless. It takes a BraveHeart to commit to the exit process and see it through to the end.

> ## Will I prepare my family and business for my exit, or will I leave it to the winds of fate?

The first step in the BraveHeart Process is to make a decision about the end result you desire. What will your transition goals be? Often, business owners don't want to address their exit because it may entail giving up control of a company they poured their life into building. It is hard for an owner to think about a business that no longer needs his expertise—or even worse, contemplate a business where he is no longer around.

Unfortunately, denial doesn't change the fact that every owner exits his business at some point. The question isn't, "Will you exit your business?" The question is, "When you exit, will you do it well?" The sooner you can accept the inevitable, the more successful the outcome can be.

Begin with the end in mind. Take advantage of the knowledge that you will exit and work toward it with intention. Create a plan that allows you to exit in a way that leaves you fully satisfied in retirement, with assets to enjoy, and a successful business that continues your legacy.

Establishing the finish line may seem like a strange place to start, but it is the most crucial part of the whole process. As Yogi Berra once said, "If you don't know where you are going, you may not get there." If you do not accept that you will eventually have to exit, you will never plan for the event, nor will you be prepared for it when it happens.

Identifying the finish line involves answering the three most fundamentally important questions of the entire exit process:

- When do I want to transition out of my business?

- To whom do I want to sell or leave my business?

- How much will I need to secure my financial independence?

As a business owner, you know that financials are vitally important, which is why most business owners start there. After all, finances are the cogs that turn the entire engine. Without a key grasp of the numbers, sales, taxes, and profits your business generates, the entire enterprise would have died long ago. You are no doubt quite comfortable with understanding the finances of your business. After all, you've spent your entire career making sure those numbers kept improving, because the financials are what ultimately drives the success of the business.

Given how important the numbers are, it may seem strange for me to suggest not to start with the financial concerns of transition. But it is not the money that determines the quality of your life—nor is it your business cash flow that determines your happiness. While money is a vital piece in the decision step, it shouldn't be your only concern, nor the one with the highest importance.

The Family Decisions

Before asking yourself how much you need to retire, or for how much you think you can sell the business, or even how you can sustain a revenue stream from your transition during retirement, ask yourself this question: How will my transition affect my family? The success of your transition and the stability of your family begin with you. It is the business leader's responsibility to initiate and oversee the entire process, acting as the lynchpin to the family's future trajectory.

Refusing to plan not only hurts the owner, but also everyone else who depends on him—employees, partners, and family. The worst-case scenario happens when the founder abdicates his responsibility and leaves it up to circumstance to decide his transition. Before you even consider exiting, it is vital that you ask yourself how your exit will affect your family, your employees, and even your community. My client Keith certainly should have.

Over the course of his career, Keith built a sprawling franchise business with nearly 100 different locations. He had three sons, but only his son John worked with Keith in the family business. Keith was a man of strong personality. He worked into his late 80s, maintaining an iron grip on the business. It was only when his health failed that he gave up operational control to John. Unfortunately, Keith not only put off training his successor but also planning for his own transition. Despite my repeated warnings, Keith never let me help him plan for his exit. Instead of taking my advice, Keith used his own lawyers to help him leave the business equally to his three sons. With one stroke of a pen, John effectively began working for his two brothers who had never spent a single day in the business.

Instead of providing a good transition and protection of family relationships, Keith created a stressful situation for all involved. This business could have been transitioned in a way that would have provided needed finances for John's retirement and ownership control of the company to John upon Keith's death. The other two sons could have been provided with a different inheritance, which had no connection to the business. Keith's poor planning has affected John and the business in many ways that Keith never foresaw or intended. Much strife could have been avoided if Keith had simply planned ahead.

When a situation like this occurs in which the current owner retains too much control with no transition plan, it can significantly degrade family relationships. I've seen members of the second generation become more and more frustrated, finally taking the situation into their own hands, when their parents resisted planning or executing any sort of succession, transition, or exit initiative. While doing so certainly gets things moving, it often alienates the parents.

Businesses (and families, for that matter) tend to succeed when people put each other's needs ahead of their own. It is an application of the Golden Rule. You don't engage in BraveHeart Planning™ just for yourself. You also do it for your family and your employees, who themselves have families depending on them. They all depend on you in some form or fashion. This planning is about caring for yourself, your family, your employees, and their families.

Relationships are a two-way street—they only work when both parties sacrifice for each other. It may benefit parents in the short run to underpay their children, and it may be easy for children to rely on their parents instead of becoming valuable to the family business, but in the long run it does irreparable damage to both the family and the business. As Zig Zigler once famously said, "You can have everything you want in life if you will just help other people get what they want."

One client in particular stands out for me in this regard. The family hired me to work with them on a BraveHeart Plan, for they wanted to do well by their many employees, their own family, and the business itself.

Jacob started a tire company shortly after the Vietnam War, with some money he was left by his grandfather. His son Jason worked for the business on holidays and in the summer while he was in high school and college. He decided to gain some outside expertise by working at another firm for five years after college. When Jason came back to work at the company, Jacob put him on a long-term management track that moved him up systematically over the years.

I was brought in to work with the family on transition planning. Shortly after I came in, Jacob turned over operational control of the business to Jason, though he stayed on board as a CEO, strategic mentor, and advisor. He also began working more on the business than in it. This is a man that values his family, his employees, and his community. He went through the breadth and depth of the BraveHeart Planning Process™ to make sure his whole family and his business would be cared for in case of his untimely death; yet he also planned for living a long time. Jacob was a business owner we could all do well to imitate.

Organizations like Jacob's demonstrate that family and business don't have to be at odds. When integrated correctly, they can be used as a leverage to boost both to heights not achievable on their own. A transition well prepared by the founder often results in financial prosperity, business sustainability, and a lasting family legacy. On the other hand, a family business transition that is handled badly can result in litigation, business collapse, family feuding, and a complete breakdown in relationships.

If you want to avoid irreparable damage to your family and legacy, it is vital that you work through Step One: The Decision, by beginning with personal questions. Before digging into the viability of your corporate value, or the trends in the mergers and acquisitions market, ask yourself: *What am I trying to accomplish with this transition?*

Have you begun to lose the fire in your belly? Have you gotten bored at work and started hunting for a new challenge or problem to which you can apply yourself? Do you see your children as potential successors who are rapidly becoming ready to lead the firm? Do you have health concerns? What about preserving your wealth in a less risky asset than private equity? All of these are vital concerns that should be considered.

The Business Decisions

The goal of engaging in the BraveHeart Planning Process™ is to leave your business to the successor you choose, on the date you want, and for the amount you need to comfortably fund your lifestyle.

Once you have settled your personal criteria and motivations for transitioning, you will next need to determine how much you will need from the transition to secure the lifestyle you desire. A 2006 survey conducted by the Employee Benefit Research Institution found that "fully 55 percent of surveyed retirees . . . said they were living in retirement on 95 percent or more of their pre-retirement income."[12] The number is even greater for business owners. Most of the clients I've worked with have maintained their standard of living and expenses, rather than decreased them. Furthermore, business owners often underestimate the amount of cash they'll need after leaving their companies. It's simply human nature to ignore hidden expenses and unforeseeable costs.

The survey by the Employee Benefit Research Institute goes on to say that more than 80 percent of retirees calculated their post-retirement needs basically off the cuff. Over half of them guessed, while others made their own estimates, read articles, or used an online calculator. Only 19 percent asked a competent financial advisor to assist them in this process.[13] Do you really want to plan for the most critical time in your life on the back of a napkin? Those who engage an exit planner to walk them through

> Do you really want to plan for the most critical time in your life on the back of a napkin?

the exit process have a huge advantage, because they have an advisor that takes into account the needs of both the owner and the business.

When setting an exit date, remember that you are just as likely to underestimate how much cash you will need, as you are to underestimate how long you will live. We are living longer and the costs of retirement are rising. As of the year 2000, men who had reached sixty-five had a 50 percent chance of living past their 85th birthday and a 25 percent chance of living past their 92nd birthday. Women have an even greater statistical chance of survival. If both spouses reach sixty-five, at least one of them has a 25 percent chance of reaching age ninety-two, while the other has a 25 percent chance of reaching age ninety-seven.[14] This survey was conducted more than fifteen years ago! Because people are living longer these days, the odds of outliving one's savings are even greater. When I was young, thirty-year retirements were rare. People saved up so that they could spend the few remaining years of their life in relative comfort and peace. These days, even a four-decade retirement is possible.

A qualified wealth manager will help you walk through these crucial calculations. He will help you determine the post-sale annual income you will need by examining retirement spending statistics and your own current spending/lifestyle habits. A qualified CPA or tax attorney will also utilize scenario planning by playing out "what if" scenarios using various net after-tax sale prices for your company. By using best- and worst-case scenarios, as well as expected returns, your team will be equipped to deal with a variety of outcomes from the business sale, and in doing so, determine how much money will be needed to invest in asset classes that will yield the net after-tax, inflation-adjusted, annual income stream you will need for the rest of your life. In essence, your future needs affect the rock bottom sale price or income stream you must have from your business in order to transition.

Obviously, the amount of income needed in retirement will vary depending on when you exit your business. Timing is of key importance. When do you want to leave? When will you be financially able to leave? Not less important is the question of when are you emotionally able to let go? Too often, I have clients approach me to help with a transition within a year of their desired exit date. It is almost always better for the owner to allow adequate time for planning. Doing so yields better results, both financially and emotionally.

A recent PricewaterhouseCoopers survey found that almost 75 percent of private enterprise owners were dissatisfied with their exit.[15] The number one reason cited for their unhappiness is the fact that they rushed the transition process. The earlier you can start preparing, the easier and less stressful your transition will be.

> ## The #1 reason for their unhappiness was because they rushed the transition process

When private equity firms invest in a company, they do so with an exit strategy already considered. Family businesses would do well to steal a page out of their playbook. Private equity firms are always looking toward the exit, always beginning with the end in mind. Family businesses should do the same. Regardless of the time horizon, a transitional exit is still the most important part of family business stability and legacy.

Thinking early about exit strategies is wise, not only to determine how much money you need from the transition, but also to determine ownership and succession issues. One of my favorite books on family transitions, *Family Business Succession,* recommends that you begin thinking about the continuity of your enterprise on the very first night you sleep peacefully, knowing you have a viable company.[16] In other words, as soon as you have made it, begin planning to leave it.

You should ask yourself a few questions: "How much do I need to secure my financial independence?" "When do I want to exit the business?"

These must come before the final question, which is, "To whom will I sell or leave my business?"

The need to realize a large cash windfall will exclude many potential successors and buyers from the pool of candidates, especially if they are insiders. The need to exit quickly may also eliminate some candidates, which is just one more reason it is so important to begin planning your exit as soon as possible. This is especially true if you are trying to transition to an employee or child. Only one-third of businesses that plan to transition to a family member actually ever do so.[17] To whom you transition your business depends significantly on your financial and personal goals, but as wildly individual as they may be, there are only a few ways to exit your business. In fact, as we see it, there are only eight ways to leave your business. They are as follows:

1. Transfer to family member

2. Sell to key employee

3. Sell using an employee stock option plan

4. Sell to co-owners

5. Sell to third party

6. Initial public offering

7. Become a passive owner and hold until your death

8. Liquidate

Some of these options will be discussed in greater detail in the three execution chapters: Transition to Children, Sale to Employees, and Sale to Third Party.

No matter what option you choose, transitioning is never an easy process, which is why so many owners put it off until it is too late. The BraveHeart Process is not for the faint of heart, but you don't have to undertake it alone.

> The BraveHeart Process isn't for the faint of heart, but that doesn't mean you have to undertake it alone

I created The BraveHeart Planning Process™ to temper my clients' optimism and address their concerns. The process will help you more accurately estimate your timing, understand the many risks involved, and err on the side of too much cash flow rather than too little. Engaging in the BraveHeart Planning Process™ may mean the difference between having a fulfilling retirement with the ability to pursue your interests or being forced to return to work because you ran out of money...only this time working for someone else.

CHAPTER 3

The Resources:

Evaluating Business and Personal Wealth

Falkland Islands, April 2, 1982

In the spring of 1982, Argentina invaded the Falkland Islands. President Leopoldo Galtieri decided his fellow Argentines needed a little boost to their nationalistic pride, and what better way than to win back long lost territory? Additionally, economic issues were brewing on the home front and Galtieri thought his country needed a diversion. His plan was simple: invade the islands just off Argentina's coast and take back their "homeland" from the far-off ruling empire, Britain.

Surprisingly, his plan initially worked. The small garrison of Royal Marines was surprised by the chutzpah of the neighboring Argentines and was forced to surrender after two days of fighting. Victory was quick and sweet.

But as with most ill-planned escapades, President Galtieri had grossly underestimated the size and scope of the British retaliation. One hundred and twenty-seven ships filled with twelve thousand men were sent under Margaret Thatcher's orders to reclaim the empire's lost lands. "Black Buck" raids began immediately with RAF Vulcan bombers lighting up nearby airstrips and Argentine ships. Mere days into the conflict, British destroyers had blown up two of Argentina's submarines, forcing the navy to retreat to its South American shores.

Nine thousand British soldiers landed on the Falkland beaches, fighting their way east until the capital city was surrounded. Six hundred British commandos would outfight twelve thousand Argentines on Mt. Kent before it was over. Encircled on land and sea, with victory wrenched from his grasp, Gen. Mario Menendez was forced to surrender the 9,800 Argentine men under his command. Three months later, President Galtieri was removed from office. The entire war lasted less than thirty days.

As foolish as it is to attack the British Empire with no provocation and no planning, it is almost as bad to try to mount an exit from your company without proper foresight. The Argentines were outmatched and outgunned, and the conflict was over almost before it had begun. If the Argentines would have sat down and taken stock of their resources, they would never have risked so much to gain so little. Counting the cost can make the difference between victory and defeat, in war and in business.

Never make large business decisions without forethought. Begin to count the cost of a transition out of your business by determining the likely value of your business should you decide to sell it. Unfortunately, this won't be easy. Putting a price tag on your business is no easy proposition, because the valuation of a private business can be as much art as science. To be fair, most things in life are hard to value; it's the reason people lose money in stocks, give away treasures at garage sales, and regret relationships only once they are gone. Though as far as businesses go, privately held entities may be the most difficult to put a price on for a variety of reasons.

Public companies are fairly simple because they are valued by the market, which is really just the court of public opinion. People toss their valuation into the ring every time they buy or sell a stock certificate. Valuations go up or down depending on a variety of factors, such as the macro economic outlook of the country and the world, foreign and domestic political stability, the health of the company itself, earnings reports, and much more.

The problem for private businesses is that there is no readily available market of millions of buyers and sellers engaging in the valuation process. Private entities are forced to estimate value based on a number of guidelines, none of which are exact. Because of the difficulty, I recommend having a professional appraiser conduct an official appraisal of your company. There are essentially four main valuation credentials offered by various credentialing entities:

- ASA – Accredited Senior Appraiser (by the American Society of Appraisers)

- CBA – Certified Business Appraiser (by the Institute of Business Appraisers)

- ABV – Accredited in Business Valuation (by the American Institute of Certified Public Accountants (AICPA))

- CVA – Certified Valuation Analyst (by the National Association of Certified Valuators and Analysts)

The most important reason to conduct an appraisal is that it helps you to determine the starting line. In our last chapter, we talked about making **The Decision**, which entailed setting the finish line so that you would know what constituted a successful exit for you personally. In this chapter, we want you to be able to set the starting line, to know where you are now so that you can successfully cross the gap to where you want to be.

In order to properly exit your business, you will need cash, and the only place that cash can come from is your business. A proper appraisal can give you an estimated price for which your business is likely to sell. Furthermore, if you intend to transfer the business to your children, an appraisal is the basis for any gift or income tax that will be levied on the transfer, depending on the strategy employed.

A business valuation is a great tool because it gives you a second opinion, one that comes from outside your business and is completely unbiased. As human beings, owners tend to overinflate the value of their enterprise. If you have ever watched a venture capital pitch, or seen the TV show *Shark Tank* on ABC, you know that startup founders often toss out million-dollar valuations before they have even made a single sale!

Seasoned owners are by no means that wildly optimistic, but whenever a person is deeply and emotionally involved in an organization, it is impossible to evaluate it completely objectively. Running an unbiased appraisal helps you to determine the feasibility of your goals. If you are planning to retire on ten million dollars, but your appraiser thinks your business is worth half that, you are in trouble. It is unlikely that buyers motivated to suppress the price would value your business double what an unbiased observer would.

Another great reason to have an appraisal conducted is to obtain information for tax planning. For most owners, the business constitutes the great majority of their wealth. By determining what your business is worth today, it allows you to plan ahead so that you can use tax saving strategies to minimize or eliminate the wealth that the IRS will suck out at the time of your transfer or death.

A valuation is also vital when designing a key employee incentive compensation plan, because it provides an objective basis for incentives. Knowing the value of your business will help you track progress as well as benchmark compensation. A wise owner will use the value of the business as a measuring rod to determine an appropriate reward system.

Finally, a business valuation is needful in the creation of value catalysts. By undergoing a valuation, you will be able to pinpoint the factors that are crucial for increasing the worth of your business. We will discuss value catalysts in detail in Chapter Five.

Owners that are looking to sell to an outside party often ask, "What's my business worth?" While this is a good question to ask, a better question is, "What is the most I can get for my business under the most favorable terms and conditions?" It is also appropriate to ask, "How can I build my business to make it worth more money in order to meet my financial goals?" Your business is worth whatever someone is willing and able to pay for it. Valuation techniques will help you determine a ballpark estimate for a sale price. This estimate will help you to plan and forecast, but it isn't until you receive your cash in the bank that you will truly know what the business is worth.

A good appraiser will utilize a number of different appraisal approaches that each emphasizes different factors, depending sometimes on the industry. The final appraisal often comes from aggregating these factors, which have varying effects on the bottom line depending on the importance of that particular approach. Once the owner receives a range of values, he can incorporate several of the most applicable techniques into an estimated average price in an attempt to arrive at an accurate valuation.

If your business is worth no more than the book value of assets, then it is worth nothing as an ongoing business entity, being nothing more than a collection of assets. If you have excess earnings above the value of your assets, however, the net present value of those earnings are generally referred to as the "going concern value."

One of the biggest factors in determining value is risk. The more risk tied up in your company, the less cash a buyer is going to be willing to shell out. If you analyze your business like any other investment, this just makes sense. The higher the risk, the higher the reward must be in order to tempt you to step further out on the risk curve. Private companies have the potential to generate huge returns, but they are also fraught with many more risks than public companies. Public companies are much more transparent, usually more established, and generally sustainable. Private companies have potential disasters lurking everywhere, at least in the minds of buyers. When it comes to interested buyers, they are going to be concerned about five key risks:

Earnings Transferability

Buyers want to know how much of the excess earnings that your business is currently making are transferable to the buyer. In other words, how much of the profits will you be taking with you when you go? Are all your earnings tied to your unique abilities? Unique abilities can include, but are not limited to, salesmanship, technical proficiency, rainmaking, and personal connections. The smaller the company, the less likely earnings are transferable. If you have little inventory, few employees, and too much oversight, the buyer is likely to reduce his offer to compensate for an inevitable loss of business when you leave.

During the value catalyst chapter, we will discuss strategies to overcome the earnings transferability risk and the owner reliance liability. For now, know that it exists and that it reduces value. The more independent you can make your business, the more it is going to be worth. You want to pump up the excess earnings capacity apart from your input as much as possible so that it doesn't rely solely on your own skills.

> The more independent you can make your business, the more it is going to be worth.

History of Profitability

Buyers want to see consistent and rising profits. It is more important to them that your cash flows are growing than that they are sizable (obviously within reason and constraints). It is also more important to them that you have consistency in earnings rather than large swings.

Once again, it is convenient to turn to the world of stock investing for an analogy. Among investors, volatility serves as a proxy for risk. In fact, in some circles, the two are synonymous. Any time you see a metric, such as standard deviation or beta, you are looking at a measure of volatility. Volatility makes price hard to predict. The more a stock price swings, the more chance you have of exiting at the wrong time, which makes the stock appear more risky.

The same goes for private companies. The more consistent your earnings are, the easier it is to predict them and the more you can count on them. Buyers want to understand what they are purchasing. If your cash flow is all over the place, it increases their chance of ending up with an asset that has cash flows die out suddenly, leaving them holding an empty bag.

Market Share—Make Your Own Game

Most closely held businesses do not dominate their market space. However, a company doesn't have to be a national entity in order to capture market share. Some regional firms are very small, yet they dominate the area in which they operate. The key is not so much the total area or market that you control but rather the force you have in your local market. As people think of the service or product that you provide, is your company the first one that comes to mind? Do you show up first in Google searches for local firms? Are you the biggest player in town?

If you are not the biggest, it is important to be the best. Instead of going toe-to-toe with a giant, you can grab market share by changing the market. Don't play by someone else's rules; make your own game. Niche it down so that you can grow it up. If you sell insurance, don't try to out mass market Mass Mutual; instead focus on a key segment, like

> **Don't play by someone else's rules; make your own game.**

disability insurance, or a unique customer, such as dentists. If the market is too big, shrink it down. If it is too wide, narrow your focus. If it is too distant, focus locally.

Industry Trends

Trends are listed next to last because they have to be rather stark in order to make a difference in valuation. If buyers see that you are in a declining industry, they are unlikely to put a premium on your business. On the other hand, if you are at the cutting edge of a red-hot growth sector, they may pay more simply due to the trajectory of the industry alone. In the late 1990s, anything Internet-related was selling for premiums of 50 to 200 P/E (price to earnings ratio). Companies that had never made a cent were selling for millions of dollars. On the other hand, no buyer would have been caught dead trying to buy into a dying industry like typewriters after computers came out. For everything in between, meaning industries that are stable like agriculture, finance, and labor, the trends are not as relevant.[18]

Unique Items

As Kevin O'Leary, from TV Show *Shark Tank*, is fond of saying, "There's nothing proprietary about your business!" Buyers are very wary of businesses that have nothing unique to offer. It introduces the risk that a larger, better-financed competitor will step into the territory and squash your business like a bug.

Generic businesses that come to mind are coffee shops, or better yet, frozen yogurt. First, anybody can open a coffee shop. They have low barriers to entry and everyone thinks they can do it. However, it is a very hard industry to make money in because it is very hard to distinguish oneself in that arena. Serving great coffee is the minimum expectation; to successfully run a coffee shop, you must create an environment that people love to be in, and more importantly, love to buy in.

Frozen yogurt (or "froyo") is another challenging business. I remember when froyo first came to my town. Everyone thought it was the coolest thing ever. The first players in the market, a firm started by three recent college grads called Fuzzy Peach, were able to grab a big market share.

Hordes of people flocked to their stores and it seemed like they were making tons of money. The problem is that everyone noticed how well they were doing. Soon, other yogurt places were popping up. It seemed like every shopping center had at least two—one on each corner. Soon, there were too many players competing for not enough customers. Most of the yogurt places are still around, but some of them went under, and it seems, from an outside perspective, as though the rest of them are not making nearly as much money as before.

Coffee and yogurt aren't the only generic businesses with no proprietary knowledge. I could say the same for the mattress industry, the furniture stores, and the electronic retailers in this town. The point is that the more proprietary technology you have, the more valuable your business will be. Even if you don't have a formal contract or long-term lease signed and sitting on your desk, you can still add value by having items unique to your business.

One of the most important ways to create value in your business is to build "customer stickiness" or customer retention. A business with clients that are unlikely to jump ship will have a huge advantage over one that has highly suspect customers. There are a number of strategies to increase customer stickiness, including contractually recurring revenue, prohibitive switching costs, and evergreen contracts.

John Brown, the founder of Business Enterprise Institute, Inc. (the developer and owner of the Certified Exit Planner Designation, or CExP), tells a story about one of his clients that was the primary printer for a local newspaper. Even though there was no formal contract in place, it would have cost the newspaper a great deal of money to switch printers, making the relationship both reliable and profitable for the printing company.

Superior Value Proposition

If you can reduce risk in your business by making your earnings transferable, showing a history of profitability, increasing market share, staying on top of industry trends, and leveraging proprietary knowledge, you will be able to make your business much more attractive than it is right now. Reducing risk is a key component of a strong valuation.

Valuation is inexact and difficult with more forecast than foresight, it is a vital piece of the BraveHeart Planning Process™. It defines the starting line, allowing the owner to clearly see where he is so that he can move to the path ahead. I strongly advise you to have a business appraisal firm value your business from an unbiased third-party perspective. Do not simply rely on your back-of-the-napkin calculations, best guesses, or "industry standards."

I often have clients tell me "Well, my firm is worth such-and-such because firms sell for five times EBITDA in my industry" (EBITDA: earnings before interest, tax, depreciation and amortization). At best, industry standards are a useful comparison tool that can be incorporated into the valuation discipline in order to anchor the valuation in market standards. At worst, supposed industry standards are misleading and an obstacle that must be overcome when presenting your firm's unique value to a perspective buyer. And yet, for all the uncertainty surrounding business value, it is usually the less problematic of the two sides of a business owner's life.

Personal Net-Worth Evaluation

Once you've accurately assessed your business assets, it's time to look on the personal side. A business owner normally has 70-90 percent of his net worth in the business! The rest would be considered personal assets, both financial and non-financial. Assessing these resources is just as important. If the business went under, what would you have left? An integral part of the BraveHeart Process is using your personal resources in a way that compliments your transition plan. Business owners often get so wrapped up in the business transition process that they forget to manage and utilize their personal assets as part of the plan.

First, it's important to create a list of major assets. Physical ownership assets include houses, cars, boats, and investment real estate. Financial ownership assets include personal retirement accounts, investment accounts, savings accounts, and insurance plans. You should also organize all of these assets by how they are registered or owned. Categorizing by ownership and registration is very important in raising issues such as estate planning gaps, transfer problems, and risk management concerns for the planners to address.

It is also important for you to understand what you have, how it is held, and why you have it. Having both spouses understand this will increase communication and help in making decisions in the planning process. Too often, you get different answers from spouses about what a certain pool of money is set aside to accomplish. This results in each spouse mentally identifying the same funds to be spent for a different purpose. Until you know what funds are held for, you cannot know whether you have as much money as you think you do! This issue can be a great source of conflict between spouses.

A friend referred to me a husband and wife who were culturally very different. The wife was Greek and the husband was German. I quickly realized that whenever they discussed money, the wife would become very expressive with both her voice and her body. The husband would just go totally silent, become stone-faced, and would literally look away from her because he could not deal with the drama. So after separating them, I discussed things with them one at a time. I realized they were talking past each other and competing for funds instead of working together.

Once I determined their assets and saw there was a pretty large pool of capital, I asked them each to write down for me how they would use the funds. After fifteen or so minutes, I took both sheets of paper, looked them over, and then gave the two spouses each other's answer sheet. I used the sheets to show them how the other viewed the money, and then I had each spouse explain how he or she came up with the list.

It became the platform from which I was able to help them do the following:

1. Understand that they did not have the money to do everything they both wanted to do

2. Realize that there were things that needed to be done for the family finances at a foundational level, which were not in yet place

3. Understand they needed to reach agreement on long-term goals, and invest accordingly for the greater good of the family

Once I got them thinking as a family instead of as two individuals, the conversation took a turn for the better. It became about listening, understanding, forgiving, and learning to love each other through how they agreed to use family funds instead of competing for what they each wanted.

It is very important to understand that you must start your planning with what you have today, not with what you once had or hope to have some day. So many people have made mistakes with investments and lost money. Others have made foolish loans to family or friends. Either way, they carry a guilt complex over it. Believe me, everyone has made financial mistakes of one kind or another. Failure is the prelude to success.

> **We all have to play the cards we hold in our hands, right now — not the ones we once had or wish to have.**

I encourage my clients to forgive themselves and others in order to deal with the reality of today, not the regrets of the past. We all have to play with the cards we hold in our hands, not those we once had or hope to have. We have to forget what lies behind and move forward with what we have now. I admit, though, that this is a much easier topic to write about than to live out. Letting go is a lesson I've learned the hard way.

Early in our marriage, my wife and I were living in Southern California. I was working at Newport Beach with a Wall Street brokerage firm and my wife was a physical therapist working with a large hospital group. We had no children, no debt, and a good amount of income. We saved quite a bit that first year of our marriage.

I had a contractor friend that lived and worked in a very nice beach town of L.A. County. We rode dirt bikes together in the mountains. He was married with a few children and he came from a fairly well-to-do family.

He asked me one evening if he could have a short-term loan. At this time, we had been friends for about a year. He said he would give it back to me within two weeks. He was just waiting on a loan to close and needed a little bridge money. I talked to my wife about it. Since we felt we knew them well, we made the loan. He gave us a pair of t-shirts with the company name emblazoned on them, just to seal the deal.

At the end of that following week, my friend began to give me excuses about why he did not have the money yet. That continued for a few months until he disappeared with our money. We never saw him or the money again. We joke now about those being the most expensive t-shirts we have ever seen...but it hurt back then and it left a bit of a scar. We could have chosen to be bitter about his betrayal and moan about the lost money forever, or we could put it behind us and move on. We decided to put it behind us and move on, but I really hadn't learned my lesson yet.

Actually, learning the lesson did not happen until many years after that first incident. I would continue making personal loans. Over and over again, they would promise to pay me back, but I never saw the money again. I think I have finally learned that I should never make a loan, but instead consider what I give to be a gift and not a loan. If the recipient wants to pay me back, that is up to them. If not, I make the gift anyway and expect no payment. Or I just decide I do not want to make a gift and say no!

Intangible Assets

Now, getting back to our discussion about working with what you have, it is important to take into consideration the intangible assets as well. What intangibles are residing within the business? Do you hold patents or have some unique processes or own some technology that is not easily reproduced?

What about the intangibles within a family? If considering an inside transition, does your successor have the talent or ability to take over the business? An accurate assessment of your successor is a key part of the resources step because a misunderstanding in this area can sideline the entire process.

In one case I worked on, the successor's talents and abilities weren't in question; rather, it was his will. Jeremy had come to see me about selling his bottling company to Glen, a key employee, for he had no children. He was so sure about Glen's abilities that he wasn't interested in having me even meet with him regarding his desire to make the purchase. However, after several months of working on the plan, I finally met with Glen.

When I sat down with him, I was surprised to find he wasn't interested in taking over the business at all! Instead, his plan was to retire within the next couple of years. He had a side business he was working on that he wanted to try to expand. He was intrigued to find the owner was planning to transition the business to him, since they hadn't ever had a conversation about it.

Needless to say, the owner was not happy. We ended up going back to the drawing board and realigning the process to work toward a sale to a third party.

The same could be said for a family transition. Parents often assume their son or daughter is going to take over the business without sitting down to talk about it! The need for honesty in this step is paramount. Regardless of your heirs' interest, do they have the capability to run the business? Do they need more schooling or time to learn the ropes? Assessing personal worth and intangible assets can be the difference between success and failure in the end.

Determining and evaluating the resources you have at your disposal is the key to formulating a winning strategy. If you do not know your financial position now, how will you know whether or not the process is successful at its conclusion? Without an accurate place to start, we cannot know how to begin or even where the finish line is. With the decision made, and the resources lined up, you can move into Step Three (The Team) in order to assemble the right group of advisors to help you get the job done.

CHAPTER 4

The Team

Paris, France, April 9, 1694

Long before Bernie Madoff created the largest Ponzi scheme in US history, a relatively unknown renegade Scots murderer fast-talked his way into the confidences of the most powerful king in contemporary history—and along the way pulled off the greatest con the world had ever seen. His name was John Law.

Law was the son of a banker but preferred extravagant pursuits—the most notable being gambling—over sober-minded finance and the family business. On April 9, 1694, he killed a man in a duel over a woman. He was convicted of murder and sentenced to death. Law was imprisoned but managed to escape to Amsterdam. Over the next several years, Law traveled throughout the continent, gambling everywhere he went. He eventually landed in the exclusive gambling clubs of Paris where he rubbed shoulders with the most powerful of the French elite, including the most powerful man on the continent: French Regent Phillippe d'Orleans.

Law was able to catch the attention of the Duke of Orleans with his brilliant financial mind and his forward-thinking economic theories. In 1720, the Duke d'Orleans appointed Law as controller general of finances, which gave Law complete mastery of the French national debt, collection of all taxes, the country's twenty-six coin mints, and most importantly, the Louisiana colony. From this power base, Law created a private corporation called the Mississippi Company, which had exclusive rights to trade with the Louisiana Colony. Law's PR campaign painted Louisiana as a veritable wonderland of riches.

The campaign paid off and company shares rocketed to over 60 times their original value, making Law the richest man in France.

Unfortunately, when the settlers recruited by Law arrived in Louisiana, they found only swamps and sickness waiting. Eighty percent of them died of tropical diseases and starvation. Naturally, word spread quickly to Paris and the shares of the Mississippi Company plunged. Angry crowds gathered outside Law's bank, throwing rocks and breaking windows. The situation became so desperate that Law fled the country. He never saw his wife and daughter again. Law escaped with his life, but left the French economy in shambles. The kingdom's finances never recovered. Louis the XV died soon after, leaving his grandson Louis the XVI in command of a bankrupt French Monarchy. Fifteen years later, the French peasantry rose up in one of the bloodiest revolutions in world history. The bloodshed would not stop until the fall of Napoleon in 1815.

When the Duke of Orleans appointed John Law as general controller of France, he had no idea his incredibly poor selection of an advisor would pave the way for the downfall of the entire French economy and rule of law. In many ways, owning a business is a bit like running a small-scale economy. Having good advisors is as important for a business owner as it is for a monarch!

In order for you to accomplish your goals, you are going to need a team that has your best interests at heart and is well-suited for your family and company needs. **The stakes are high—the majority of your net worth is at stake.** This is extremely important, because the quality of advisors selected can make or break the exit plan. The bigger the business being transitioned, the wider and deeper a team's knowledge and experience need to be. The stakes are high; the majority of your net worth is at stake. As a result, you need high caliber professionals to make sure the transition is a success.

You will want to choose an exit planner with a deep and wide background across a variety of disciplines. I could see early in my career how much the fields of finance, tax, insurance, and law crossed over. Most practitioners work in one or two areas, but I saw how much value someone that could see the whole picture could add. I started out as a stockbroker but knew

I needed more education to better serve the clients, so I obtained a CFP designation. After that, I could see still more need for education, which is why I decided to go to law school.

My education didn't stop with law school. I wanted to be able to help integrate business planning, estate planning, and wealth management, so I decided to earn my exit planning certification (CExP). I wanted to care for my clients so that all the hard work they put in during their lives wasn't wasted when they died through estate taxes, business failure, or family conflict. I wanted to make sure that not only would they build a legacy, but they would also be able to protect it. I was tired of working with clients to get the beginning and middle of their careers right, only to see their financial security botched by a poorly planned exit. Your exit is the single most critical point in your career, which is why I have made it the focus of mine.

Before we get into specific team member roles, it is time to step back and ask yourself, *Why should I use advisors in my business transition?* After all, you are a very successful businessperson who is always charge and intimately involved in all the details of your business. You no doubt have vast experience brokering deals, buying and selling equipment, moving inventory, and much more. Your competence at running your business cannot be questioned, so why wouldn't you be qualified to sell it? Or at the very least, why couldn't you engineer your own transition? Good advisors do not come cheap; the more qualified and skilled they are, the more money they charge.

While price is an issue, we will address that valid concern last. The problem with running your own transition is that the skills needed to run a business are very different from those needed to transition it. You have done an excellent job working in and on your business, but if you are like most owners, you have never sold a business or drafted an estate plan. Simply put, the highest and best use of your time and talents is not in selling a business or planning a transition, nor do you likely have the breadth and depth of experience that your advisors will have. Besides, you don't have the time to do everything by yourself. Your energy is devoted to running a business, and that's where it belongs.

Furthermore, unless you have spent half a lifetime earning professional degrees, it is unlikely that you have all the knowledge needed to run a transition. The team members described in the following pages have devoted their entire careers to each of their specialties. They know the ins and outs of tax law, marketing, insurance products, investment management, mergers and acquisitions best practices, succession issues, and much more. It is impossible for a single person to know the intimate details of such varied and complex disciplines as the ones involved in the BraveHeart Process. Take my word for it. I have counseled hundreds of businesses; you are going to need the services of experts whose education, training, and experience will supplement your own so that you can make informed decisions in order to achieve your exit objectives.

A new client named Cameron came to see me some years ago to ask us about managing money for him and to see if we might be able to help him handle some transfers of assets to children in a tax efficient manner. As I began working with him, he told me the story of how he had handled the sale of his company a year or so ago. At first, he told me the story with pride, but after I began to ask questions his pride began to wither. The more I learned and probed, the more embarrassed he became.

He had a CPA who had worked with him for many years. He also had a general practice lawyer, who had handled some unlawful detainers to get rid of deadbeat tenants and had done simple estate planning for him. Both of these guys were his friends, so when he decided to sell the company, he sought advice from both of them.

The advice conflicted somewhat. Instead of resolving the discrepancies, he decided to take part of the advice from each. He felt that since he had run a successful company for many years, he could also handle the sale, and so he did. It was clear from his discussion that neither the CPA nor the lawyer understood anything about preparing for a sale or running an auction process. They also knew little about exit planning.

Cameron's method of trying to take advice from different professionals to create his own plan turned into a mess. The professionals with whom he worked also did not advise him to get the kind of help he needed. He did get his sale completed, but there was nothing to brag about. The value he came up with for the company was flawed and at least 50 percent low. He decided to trust himself to make decisions about things for which he had no expertise. As a result, he missed opportunities to plan for his family and benefit long-term employees, and he left a lot of money on the table. He did make the buyer very happy and he did save some professional fees. But you do tend to get what you pay for.

A successful exit team needs to have, at the very least, an exit planner, an accountant, and an attorney. For businesses worth at least $5,000,000-$10,000,000, an M&A consultant, an estate planning attorney, a business attorney, and an insurance specialist are also needed. If qualified, the accounting firm may handle the business appraisal portion of the plan, but if not, you will also need a valuation expert on your team.

Patrick M. Foley, of Baird Capital, recommends using the professionals that other professionals would use.[19] Foley explains that in every industry, there are a handful of top practitioners that other people in the same line of work will go to when they need help. Foley recommends that your exit team be composed of these professionals. He likens the top exit practitioners to the surgeon that other doctors trust to operate on them, the lawyer other lawyers call when they've got a problem, and the bartender other bartenders order their Long Island Ice Teas from.

The only problem with Mr. Foley's advice is that as an outsider, it is incredibly difficult to find out who these people are. Patients don't normally know who the top surgeon is in a hospital. All they can see are the marketing efforts of each doctor. They aren't privy to the inner workings of his office, nor can they interact with all the patients of every surgeon in town. The only thing a patient can really know is how well their own surgery went...and that is only after the fact! So how does one solve this trust problem—what economists would call the asymmetric information issue? How does one select the very best of the best for his exit team without having the expertise to differentiate between the so-so practitioners and the truly exceptional? That's exactly where the exit planner comes in.

In my opinion, one of the most important duties of the exit planner is to bring together an all-star team of advisors. The exit planner should help you assemble a team of advisors that are well-respected in their particular fields, and that have a nice fit with that particular business owner. Business owners only get one shot at transitioning so I believe they should get as much talent as possible on their side of the court.

Experienced exit planners have worked with hundreds of professionals. As a result, they have learned what to expect from advisors on a team and how to motivate them to give their best and to communicate effectively.

The Business Team

The exit planner (Who is called the "BraveHeart Planner" when our process is being utilized) is the one who puts the plan in motion, monitors progress, brings the team together, acts as the owner's primary representative, and facilitates the sale or transition process. He stands by the owner's side every step of the way to make sure he crosses the finish line a winner.

As such, the exit planner's primary role is to coordinate the entire process; helping you bring in key players. If you have chosen to exit via a third-party sale he must help you prepare the company for sale, help hire the M&A firm when the time is right, manage your expectations, and walk with you through the whole turbulent process. A third-party sale process is a challenge and involves much preparation and hard work. It can take years and it can also give you quite a ride on your own emotional roller coaster. The deal will usually get dropped in the ditch a few times before it is completed. If you are selling outside be prepared for a process fraught with complexity and awash in high-pressure decision-making.

In addition to the exit planner, you will also need two to three lawyers. Whether you like lawyers or not, you need them on your exit team. They will address two vital areas: the sales transaction and the structure of your estate. For these two functions, you will need at least one M&A lawyer and one estate planning lawyer on your attorney team.

The estate planning lawyer will need to be one of the first professionals to consider as you begin planning. There are certain strategies and planning opportunities that must be completed for the family estate plan before you even contemplate a sale. This is one of the primary reasons why the BraveHeart Planning Process™ can take a number of years and should not be rushed, especially for a family whose wealth is in excess of $10 million dollars. For at that value you begin to need some estate tax planning.

You also need an estate planning lawyer to examine trust and gifting options for the family. If planning is timely, he may even create strategies to remove part of the business interests from your estate, if necessary. He will also need to review existing buy-sell agreements and make sure they are in line with your plans. The size of the law firm engaged depends on the need for specialized local knowledge or national firepower.

Before you put your company up for sale, or even prepare for a transition, you will need your business lawyer to conduct a legal audit of all your existing operations so that you know everything is legally in order before the process begins. He will review shareholder agreements, minutes, articles, bylaws, compensation plans, and any other legal arrangements the company might have. He may also recommend a patent attorney to review the intellectual property of the company. This will help to head off any problems that could occur down the line when the buyer reviews your documentation.

You will also want to hire an M&A lawyer with deep experience in transactions. Someone with expertise in transactions will catch details that other attorneys would miss. He will also be helpful in the negotiation process during a sale, acting as your advocate, as well as working on completing the sale contract or other contracts needed in an insider transition.

The next player on your team needs to be a competent accounting firm that can provide strong tax advice. Financials are incredibly important to the sale process as acquirers will be thoroughly reviewing all business financial records. Because of the due diligence that naturally accompanies a sale, the sooner an accounting firm is involved, the better. A good M&A firm will have strong accounting skills to be able to help the CPA firm get the financials in shape and ready for the sale. Buyers want to know every gritty detail of the company they are buying, so you can expect a thorough due diligence process.

Being prepared for this process will not only make the sale process easier for you, but it should also help you get a better price. Issues found in due diligence often reduce the sale price, sometimes retroactively. I have found that buyers tend to utilize the due diligence process to deliberately drive down the purchase price. The best case scenario for the buyer is that the issues don't come out until near the closing when the seller is already mentally and emotionally committed to the sale and so willing to accept a change in price and terms with little objection.

I recommend that every business owner who plans to sell to a third party conduct a pre-sale due diligence process with his accounting firm and business law firm before a buyer looks at even a single financial document. The accounting portion of the presale due diligence is known as a quality of earnings review. The business law firm will need to do a legal audit of your company.

In some circles, this pre-sale preparation is known as reverse due diligence. It is a detailed review of your statements that acts as a warm up for the due diligence conducted by the potential buyer. By being proactive, you can identify issues and minimize potential risks that could derail the deal later on. A problem that can be discovered and fixed before the buyer finds out will guarantee a smoother ride.

Clear reporting will go a long way towards facilitating the exit or transition process. Clean books are a sign of a well-run organization. Buyers will take it as a piece of reassurance that they can have confidence in what they are buying. In addition to reporting, accountants also often provide business valuations, audits, and normalization of financial statements. You will need to become familiar with these terms when it comes time to plan for your own sale and you will need to make sure your accountant is competent to do this kind of work.

We discussed valuation in the last chapter, so I am not going to dive into it here. For larger transactions, audits are imperative because buyers put a whole lot more faith in books that have been audited by a trustworthy accounting firm than those that haven't. Depending upon the size of the business, a full audit may be excessive. A lower level of CPA attestation is probably sufficient on smaller deals. Equally important though, is a history (at least three years) of reviews or audits.

Normalizing financial statements involves examining the true cash flows of a business by adding back in above-market salaries, fringe benefits, unusual expenses, and other items that obscure true value for the buyer.

Essentially, what you are doing when you recast your financial statements is allowing a potential buyer to see what they would be getting without you around. Owners often use their businesses (and rightly so) to further their own tax and personal goals. By normalizing your statements, you are showing buyers how much the business is really worth and what the real cash flows look like, apart from your influence on the books.

M&A consultants are a useful asset on most exit teams. They will represent you in the sale, unless your company is smaller. Business brokers usually sell companies purchased by individuals, wherein the sale of the business is less than $5 million. Investment bankers typically work with businesses worth $5 million or more in value. The size and complexity of your deal should determine what kind of advisor you hire and what location you should hire from.

The primary responsibilities of an M&A consultant include:

- Providing advice on deal structure and ways to improve the attractiveness of your business

- Analyzing the marketplace in terms of transaction activity, market trends and other factors that impact the price you'll likely receive

- Seeking and screening potential buyers, whether among competitors, investors or companies seeking a strategic fit

- Negotiating with potential buyers on your behalf

The Family Team

The financial world is big, complex, and involves too many moving parts for you to master it all on your own. You need a team. Furthermore, no one possesses the entire skill set needed to properly service those with high net worth. As a result, hiring a competent team of professionals with deep backgrounds across a range of financial specialties is paramount. At the very least, you must have one in each of the following categories:

Private Client Lawyer

Private client lawyers can address different types of tax, estate planning, and business legal needs. A very good business law and estate planning firm can provide business and tax advice that will save you money in more ways than you can imagine. That includes income taxes and estate taxes. They can also help set up your estate to survive and minimize taxes for generations.

Personal Accountant

Hire a good CPA firm known for their tax-planning prowess to make specific recommendations to mitigate tax liabilities and help with accounting organization. They will also help you with organization of your affairs in many ways. That is who they are—good record-keepers. However, we also want you to have awesome planners to go along with that record-keeping skill set. One big caution: remember that your records, held by your CPA, are essentially open to the IRS. If there is sensitive information that you do not want showing up somewhere else, save that information to share with your lawyers, for they have attorney/client privilege. This privilege protects certain communications between a client and his or her attorney and keeps those communications confidential. This is not about cheating the buyer, for you will have to make full disclosure, but about protecting information that should have no bearing on the sale.

Taxes are inevitable. They are as constant as death and consistent as sunrise. Rates and amounts will change, but one thing remains the same: you will never escape taxes. They will follow you wherever you go, whether you buy goods, earn income, or invest money. You can't even die in peace without the government taking its share! So determine to play the game and hire good tax counsel.

Personal Insurance Professional

You need to hire insurance professionals who can identify and structure a plan that leverages the entire range of property, casualty and life insurance products to protect risks in multiple areas. If you are worth more than a few million dollars, you should look for firms that are able to write property/casualty insurance with some of the higher end companies. These higher end companies include ACE Group, The Chubb Group, PURE (Privilege Underwriters Reciprocal Exchange), and AIG Private Client Group. Those are some of the companies that your agent should be able to offer you, as evidence of his ability to service your needs. These companies are dedicated to assessing, reducing and managing risk proactively for higher net worth families. They provide concierge level service for your insurance coverage and are especially valuable during a claim.

Wealth Manager

You will need a wealth management firm or a multi-family office that can provide investment management and other services for you and your family. At my company, Long Family Office, we provide wealth management services to high net-worth clients. We would generally describe them as family stewards.

CEG Worldwide is the #1 coach for top financial advisors. I am part of "The Roundtable" that is CEG's Graduate School of Elite Financial Advisors. This is an invitation-only program.

CEG typically defines wealth management as a formula:

$$WM = IC + AP + RM$$

To translate: wealth management equals investment consulting plus advanced planning plus relationship management.

IC = investment consulting. This is the management of all investment elements to maximize the likelihood that clients will achieve what is financially important to them. IC includes risk evaluation, asset allocation, portfolio performance analysis, assessment of impact of taxes, and investment policy statement.

AP=advanced planning, which has its own formula definition: $AP = WE + WT + WP + CG$. Advanced planning equals wealth enhancement (tax mitigation and cash flow planning) plus wealth transfer plus wealth protection (risk management, legal structures and risk management) plus charitable giving.

RM = relationship management. This is management of the client relationship and the relationship of the professional network supporting the client.

It is important to work with a firm that will not only invest your money, but can also provide you with a robust menu of services to take care of the many financial needs of your family.

Exit Planner

BraveHeart Planning™ includes exit planning (as we practice it), which is unique to my firm. However, the basics of the exit planning portion of what we do comes from the process developed by my friend, attorney John Brown, and his company, Business Enterprise, Inc. (BEI). (I earned my certified exit planning credential through this organization some years ago.) I would have you consider using an advisor that has the certified exit planner (CExP) credential from Business Enterprise, Inc. of Denver, Colorado. That should assure you that they are well trained and have the resources of BEI behind them to assist you in your exit plan.

There are a few other designations that are available to those interested in exit planning, but these designations are given after one to five days of classroom instruction. They do not come close to the months of rigorous study and academic requirements of the CExP. While the other credentials would be better than nothing, my advice is to stick with those holding the CExP if possible. You should also consider the background of the planner with whom you work. Has planning been part of their career, such as also being a CPA, attorney, certified financial planner, or a chartered life underwriter? That kind of experience is likely necessary to strengthen the validity of your choice for the CExP credential holder.

You will need a professional that can take the 30,000-foot view of your whole financial life and make the best choice by integrating each part. This is someone that understands the big picture on estate planning, taxes, investing, risk management, business planning, and etc. That person need not be an expert in all these fields, but he or she must be willing to "issue spot" and bring a team together to integrate the planning for the family and the business. Your BraveHeart advisor/exit planner is going to be vitally important because he will work on both the business and the personal sides of your life. He will take the role of big picture issue spotter and coordinate the work of the various professionals on behalf of the family to produce a unified approach to your overall wealth management plan and exit plan.

Not only is it important that you assemble a team—as the tasks required to build a strong financial future for your family are both complex and time-consuming—but it is also important that you select individuals who are competent in their respective fields, able to communicate with each other, and ultimately, able to work together. You very much want the team coordinating and cooperating in order to formulate the best course of actions and the best outcomes for the business and the family.

Many of the best exit planners may already have a top-notch team of other professionals they trust and with whom they regularly work. But each professional should be considered based on these six key characteristics.

1. Character/A Wonderful Reputation

Don't ever work with someone whose character you question, because you will regret it. The world is filled with financial advisors, lawyers, insurance agents, and CPAs, but it is incredibly difficult to determine what separates a good one from a bad one, at least until it is too late. You won't know how adequate your insurance protection is until you need it, you won't be able to measure the risk in your portfolio until the market plunges, and you won't ever know how well your estate plan was constructed because you will be gone by the time it is implemented. Given that the only way you will know good work is in hindsight, it is vital that you work with someone you can trust.

2. Chemistry/Works Well with Others

It is important to have chemistry with the professionals in your life. They are going to be making important recommendations about your life—if you don't like them, it's going to be tough to take their advice.

3. Caring/Genuinely Cares for Their Clients

Care and competence are essential together. Advisors that are competent, but not caring may make careless mistakes, while someone incompetent, but caring is likely to make unconscious ones.

4. Competence/Experienced and Well Considered by Peers

As I mentioned before, I recommend using the professionals that other professionals would use. The financial industry especially is full of fast talkers with an alphabet soup of titles. Some degrees are better than others (my firm tends to respect financial practitioners that have the CFA, CFP, CLU, CHFC, or CPA designations). Remember that every industry has a handful of top practitioners that other people in the same line of work will go to when they need help. An exit planner can help you find those advisors.

5. Cost-effective/Sensible Fees

Cost effective does not mean cheap; it means valuable, based on the money spent. All of the advisors on your team are going to be expensive if they are any good at all; you just need to make sure they are worth the cost.

6. Consultative/Works in a Consultative Manner[20]

The scope and breadth of the work required in exit planning precludes the possibility of one person being qualified to do all of the work. We have only listed some of the professionals that could be called upon to assist you, as you move through your own exit planning process.

7. Willing to Advise

Finally, hire professionals who are willing to advise you, not just do their jobs. The best professionals don't merely go through the motions; they actively seek opportunities to strengthen your planning. Your

> **Finally, hire professionals who are willing to advise you, not just do their jobs.**

professionals should work in a consultative way. They need to ask questions and listen carefully to what is important to you, including the life vision you have for yourself and your family. They should recommend what they believe is appropriate for you after deeply understanding your particular situation.

Big Picture Considerations

All of your advisors should expect to be part of a team and not try to isolate you from other advisors. That kind of conduct should be a red flag for you. If they do not want to work with any other advisors, it may be because they have an agenda that they intend to impose on you, or they are afraid that others may discover that they really don't know what they are doing. Either way, you end up with a mess. The best mix is to find an advisor who is constantly looking out for your well-being, works collaboratively with other professionals and has the expertise to help you make wise decisions for you and your family.

The beauty of BraveHeart Planning™, as we practice it, is that you have the ability to observe the planning and implementation as the case progresses. You don't just get a plan to put on a shelf. Instead, you have planning completed and then executed as you go along. It is an experience that you control. Make sure your advisor who is acting as the exit planner is guiding you in implementation and not just providing a plan that gathers dust.

Your advisors should advise you and prepare you for the day when the transition planning is executed. Assuming your transition includes a sale, it can be hard to learn to live with suddenly liquid wealth and the free time that comes with it. Both new money and a huge amount of free time can provide challenges that could be difficult to handle without adequate preparation. To some this may sound silly, but many who are unprepared have stumbled on this part of their life when they expected it to be the best part.

> **A successful transition will strengthen family ties.**

Finally, it's important to see your family members as team players. Many business transitions have gone awry because the spouse wasn't on board with the process or thought it should be handled another way. A strong spousal relationship can be a key asset for the exit process, giving helpful perspective on major decisions that must be made. A successful transition should strengthen family ties, not break them.

I remember a transaction I worked on many years ago with a family that was selling their business to a third party. The husband assured me that his wife did not need to be included in any of our discussions, despite my objections. He stood his ground, completely convinced that all she needed to do was sign her name at the close, so we moved forward without her.

The day of the closing came around and my conference room was packed with lawyers. My client sat in front of a long table filled with documents. We had been through an emotional sale process and everything was all settled when the wife came storming in. She marched right up to the head of the table and declared she wasn't signing anything because not a single person had consulted her during the entire process. The husband's refusal to include his wife put the deal back an entire month, resulted in thousands of dollars of extra legal fees, and almost cost him the sale.

Securing familial buy-in early is essential to creating a team-like atmosphere throughout the transition. Keep the end in mind: when the process is over, retirement will be much more enjoyable if your spouse has been happy the entire time! Keep your spouse and key family relations not just in-the-know, but also a part of the larger decisions that are bound to come your way throughout the BraveHeart Planning Process™.

CHAPTER 5

Value Catalysts

May 16, 1940

World War One was the war to end all wars. Raging for four and a half brutal years, the Great War devastated Europe. Soldiers on both sides were put through hell—fighting through freezing winters, scorching summers, long nights, empty stomachs, and pain and misery on a scale never before seen. By the end of the war, over nine million men had been killed, with another twenty-one million wounded. The country of France was literally decimated, with around 11 percent of its population killed or wounded. The French high command vowed that never again would they face such misery. They would not ever be unprepared for war with Germany again.

Influenced by their experiences in WWI, the French established a line of concrete fortifications, obstacles, and weapons installments along the border with Germany, Luxembourg, and Switzerland known as the Maginot Line. The strategy behind the Maginot Line was distinctly informed by the success of static defensive warfare in the previous war. In World War One, the French achieved victory by digging in and throwing up trenches, slowly and surely wearing down the German offensive until it ground to a standstill. The Maginot Line followed that strategy by seeking to stop the Germans before they could even set foot on French soil.

French military experts called the Maginot Line a work of genius. They believed it would allow the French army enough time to mobilize for any conflict coming their way. The Maginot Line truly was a feat of engineering. It was impregnable to most forms of attack available at the time, including aerial bombings and tank fire. The fortifications had state-of-the-art living conditions for garrisoned troops, air conditioning, comfortable eating areas, and underground railroads. Yet for all of its wonderful accommodations and impervious defenses, the Maginot Line was a strategic disaster.

The military generals of the German army knew their business well. Instead of attacking the line directly, the Germans simply went around it. Hitler ordered his Panzer divisions to bulldoze straight through the Ardennes forest and the Low Countries in a move the French thought impossible. German Blitzkrieg tactics caught the French completely off guard, forcing the army to surrender in a matter of weeks. Within a month and a half, the entire country of France was in German hands.

The French believed they were making investments that counted, but in the end, true value would have been found in modern equipment, planes, and armored artillery rather than outdated concrete walls. The Germans invested heavily in modern technology and as a result smashed through French defenses. The Germans, not the French, built what mattered. The value catalysts the French ignored cost them their freedom.

"Value catalyst" (VC) is a term I've coined to describe structures and strategies that have a disproportionate impact on organizations. You will hear other speakers and authors talk about value drivers or business drivers, but I find the terms too constraining. Value catalysts are not limited to business, and they do not just create more zeros on the end of a sale price. A value catalyst (VC) is a process or person that creates more energy, time, or money than it takes in. It is a broader category than simply sale price tactics. Catalysts in chemical reactions spark change. They jumpstart a chain of events, and the same is true of VCs. Implementing VCs can truly change the direction of your business and the quality of your life.

Value catalysts are the structures, people, and processes that help owners work on their business instead of in it. Effective VCs are the difference between true owners and glorified managers. Do you have a business that can run well without you? Suppose you were to leave for six months for any reason at all, including vacation, sickness, travel, side ventures. Would your business survive? If you have any hesitation answering that question in the affirmative, it is unlikely that your business has the VCs it needs. Self-sustaining businesses sell for much higher multiples than those that rely on one, or a few key employees.

Businesses that are in the midst of transition are not the only ones that benefit from value catalysts. All businesses are created to build value for their owners. In this chapter we will explore the VCs that make the most difference in both business and family. The key to growing a more valuable business and a stronger family is investing in VCs that last for the long term.

Managing the Business as an Investment

Few business owners manage their business wealth with the same expertise and advice as they do their liquid investments, such as their pension plans or trust accounts.

They should reconsider. The reason that most owners are caught flat-footed when tragedy strikes, or the unthinkable happens, is that they do not think of their business as an investment, at least not in the big picture context of their total financial life. Have you ever considered what your investment allocation in your investment portfolio would look like if you added in the stock of your privately-owned business? Seemingly diversified portfolios are misleading without the inclusion of private equity—the individual's ownership of a private company.

> Few business owners manage their business wealth with the same expertise and advice as they do their liquid investments.

Leaving your business out of your portfolio calculations is a terrible mistake because it skews your perception of the risk to which you are exposed. You may think that you are safely invested in 60 percent bonds, 10 percent cash, and 30 percent globally diversified public stocks (or whatever your portfolio allocations happen to be), but that is not the entire truth. In reality, you are likely to have 70 percent to 90 percent of your total wealth tied up in your business.

According to Mercer Capital, households with private equity interest invest more than 70 percent of their wealth in a single private company in which they have active management interests. Another shocking statistic is that 75 percent of the total private equity market is owned by people who invest more than half of their net worth in private equity. Simply put: the wealth of high net worth Americans is extremely concentrated in private equity. The crazy thing about this incredible concentration of wealth is that private equity returns are on average no higher than market return on all publicly traded equity.[21]

Private equity, whether it is your own business or someone else's, has a much higher risk profile than bonds, cash, or even public stocks. Are you taking that risk into account when you make personal and investment decisions?

The risk problem is addressed in a nifty little read titled *The 1 Percent Solution,* thusly named because the author, Chris Mercer of Mercer Capital, suggests that the solution to this huge risk perception gap lies in treating your ownership interest as an investment. Mercer suggests that as a business owner, you should consider allocating an equally proportionate budget to managing your pre-liquid wealth as you do to managing your liquid wealth.

Mercer Capital defines private equity wealth as "pre-liquid" because these assets either become liquid or facilitate the creation of liquid assets when they are sold (entire businesses or partial sales) or when they distribute cash to their owners. The problem is that owners tend not to think of their business as pre-liquid wealth and therefore do not take steps to build its value.

Investors, whether they are very wealthy, wealthy, affluent, or even middle class, all tend to treat their liquid assets like an investment. They place the funds in the custody of capable investment managers that handle direct investment activities and periodic changes to the portfolios. These asset managers, if they have any training of any value at all, will set objectives, establish strategies, regularly monitor investments, and regularly review and reallocate investment capital as needed.

Owners of businesses, however, have no such process for managing their private equity investment. They perhaps set objectives for their business, and they possibly establish strategies for growth and income, but almost no privately-held businesses constantly monitor progress and risk or work to enhance the investment asset, and they certainly don't regularly review the investment. Despite the fact that pre-liquid assets make up the bulk of wealthy Americans' wealth, very few wealth managers are involved in setting investment objectives for substantial pre-liquid assets held by their clients.

In many cases, wealth managers attempt to help clients without specific knowledge of the largest single asset in their clients' portfolio. When clients obtain liquidity from a privately-held business, they may seek larger and more sophisticated wealth managers for newly-obtained liquidity, but fail to find the same expertise when seeking a transition from their business.

Business owners naturally accept that management of liquid assets will have a price, yet they often balk at paying a fee for business management services. A million dollars in managed, liquid funds is likely to cost around 1 percent on average for the services of your asset managers. However, most owners refuse to pay even a fraction of this percentage to manage their pre-liquid wealth, despite the fact that pre-liquid wealth is much more complex and difficult to manage, not to mention more important.

> The *One Percent Solution* offers an intriguing thought: just as you spend 1 percent of your liquid portfolio to manage it, what if you spent 1 percent of your private business wealth to enhance its overall value?

The One Percent Solution offers an intriguing thought: Just as you spend 1 percent of your liquid portfolio to manage it, what if you spent income equal to 1 percent of your private business wealth to enhance its overall value? In a closely-held or family business worth $20 million, the budget for managing that wealth might be about $200,000 (or about $100,000 if you use half a percent as your "management fee" percent). If the business is worth less than $20 million, Mercer recommends allocating 1 percent to 2 percent to the budget for its management.

Managing pre-liquid wealth can come with a pretty big sticker price. As an owner, however, you know that the question to ask is not "How much will it cost me?" but rather, "What value will it bring to me?" Anything you implement in a business must contribute to the bottom line or insure the survivability of the business. At the end of the day, every decision, big or small, must be evaluated on the criteria of value. Will it enhance the business value and its cash flows or will it detract from them?

If your company is of a sufficient size, one percent can be a substantial chunk of change. What will this sizable allocation be spent on? Your budget could include:

- Wealth manager compensation

- Annual valuations and monitoring of value growth

- Buy-sell agreements

- Life insurance funding

- Estate planning

- Financial planning

- Annually audited financial statements

- Annual legal review

- Other "make-ready" projects

- Exit or transition planning

I've said it before and I'll say it again: Most business owners just work in their businesses; those who consider ownership positions to be investments also regularly work *on* their businesses. One percent is not cheap, but it is worthwhile. Investment management expenses are not free, but these fees are worth every penny when returns are enhanced, especially when returns are great enough to more than offset expenses. The same could be said about pre-liquid business managers. When the transition is complete and your retirement is much more secure, you will thank yourself for having the foresight to invest in the enhancement of your business's position in the marketplace.

Exit planning falls within the definition of spending money towards managing your business and pre-liquid wealth. I have encountered countless owners that have tried to run their own sale or transition or that have tried to hire professionals (who tend to be unqualified for exit planning) for far less than is required to do a decent job. The only problem is that in life you often get what you pay for.

Many times though, the problem is not stubbornness or cheapness, but simply ignorance. Most owners don't manage their pre-liquid wealth because they do not know what that would look like. Owners of small to mid-sized businesses especially often don't know what they don't know. The skill set needed to start a business is different from those needed to run it, which is in turn different than those needed to transition it. I created the BraveHeart Planning Process™ in part to give family business owners a guide to managing their pre-liquid wealth with wisdom and insight. I do not want family businesses to face the coming tsunami of transitions unaware or unprepared.

Managing the pre-liquid wealth in private companies involves creating strategies for converting that wealth from pre-liquid to liquid form over time through enhanced performance, distributions, partial sales, and ultimately the sale or transition of a business. Part of managing pre-liquid wealth is incorporating it into the household's total portfolio, which should emphasize both public and private equity.

In essence, it requires focus on managing your total wealth, not just your liquid wealth. I've watched too many owners run their business into the ground by staying in a dying industry or growing too fast and then collapsing. I've seen owners pull off a huge sale with more than adequate funds only to watch them blow the money on overly risky investments after the sale. Don't do that to your family. Treating your business like an investment will help you protect your family. And, as soon as possible, insulate your loved ones' financial security from the welfare of the business. You want your family to be taken care of no matter what happens in the business.

Business Value Catalysts

A goal of every owner is to create more value in his business, which often translates into creating more cash flow. The value of your business determines not only the quality of your life once you leave your company, but also how long it will take for you to be ready to leave, based on your goals. Creating the value you want may take years of effort. Too many owners just work in their business instead of on it. When you think of it that way, most small business owners are really just glorified managers. They are technicians who know how to do their job really well, but they never build a company that can live without them. They are the company.

> These actions are the secret sauce – differentiating businesses that sell for outrageous prices and those that end up in fire-sale auctions.

According to Deloitte and Touche, LLP, more than 71 percent of small and mid-sized enterprise owners plan on exiting their business in the next ten years,[22] yet few organizations genuinely understand what actions they must take to achieve this goal. These actions are the secret sauce, which differentiate businesses that sell for outrageous prices and those that end up in fire-sale auctions. Buyers are looking for key indicators of value. They don't want businesses that will collapse when the owners leave. They look for characteristics of longevity. At Long Business Advisors, we call these features "value catalysts." They are the defining characteristics that transform a good business into a great one.

Value catalysts jump start success. They turn mildly profitable businesses into moneymaking machines. They are the key difference between a technician that builds an operation around his talents and an owner that understands how to multiply his knowledge and systematize it.

Value catalysts are the lynchpin to creating a successful exit. The key to a great exit is preparation, and that is what VCs are all about. Buyers pay top dollar prices for businesses that they perceive to be valuable, not just ones with good EBITDA. Purchasers are going to look much deeper than a P&L (profit and loss); they are going to look for attributes that reduce their risk and increase their return. Just like clinching any kind of sale, from ice cream bars to insurance, story-telling is the key to landing a great price for your business. It is vital that your business tells a story of stability and growth, both in the past and in the future.

Building VCs starts long before you intend to exit. For this reason, we recommend beginning the BraveHeart Planning Process™ now, or at least five to ten years before your planned exit. Some changes you make to your business in order to facilitate the reduction of your tax burden have to be made ten years before a transition. On top of the tax ramifications, many of these VCs take time to get off the ground (as we will see shortly).

You are intimately aware of how long and how much effort it takes to start a business. What you may not realize is that taking it to the next level will require almost as much. Late is better than never, but the sooner you begin, the better.

Value catalysts consist of things like:

- Stable and motivated management team

- Operating systems that sustain the growth of the business

- An established and diverse customer /supplier base

- Recurring revenue

- Realistic growth strategies

- Strong financial controls

- Proprietary technology or systems, customized know-how growth in cash flow, profitability, revenue and sales

- Avoiding reliance on 1-2 key sales people or product design people

Buyers seeking to acquire your business will look at these key metrics when determining a value they are willing to pay. Businesses without value catalysts represent huge risks for acquirers.

Stable and Motivated Management

> **The single most important Value Catalyst is your management team.**

The single most important value catalyst in your business is your management team. It is from this one catalyst that all others flow. None of the items listed above can be enacted on your own. You need a management team that you can rely on, that can eventually run the business without you. It takes a team—a well-oiled and disciplined team—to implement strong VCs and keep them working consistently to increase the value of your business.

Because the management team is the most important catalyst, we will spend the most time on it. This team includes the people who are responsible for setting and implementing the company's strategic direction, aligning strategic objectives with the mission and vision of the company, monitoring and controlling high-level activities with the business plan, and finally motivating and supervising the workforce.

Most small companies fold all these responsibilities into a single role: that of the executive/owner/manager/chairman/the man. While this can work and work well for a small organization, it is not even remotely scalable, and it retards the company's growth. If you have built your entire company around your own skills and expertise, you can make good money, but the company is never going to grow beyond you. You will end up having trouble selling or transitioning for a good price because there will be nothing for buyers to buy. Once you leave, the business will fold.

Bruce ran a large cattle operation in the Central Coast of California. He ruled with an iron fist and his style was micromanagement. Though he had a son that worked for him, he refused to surrender other than menial decisions to him. Art was a hard worker and a loyal son, but he did not want to confront his dad, for he respected him and feared him.

Bruce was a difficult man to be around, though successful and clearly driven. And of course, he continued to be healthy and worked daily into his late 80s. While the work kept him engaged into old age, he managed his cattle operation in ways that slowly made Art bitter. Because Bruce considered himself irreplaceable, he refused to cede decision-making to Art. Since he did not teach decision-making skills to Art, he did not trust him to make decisions. Therefore Bruce would not, and (in his mind) could not, delegate to him.

As an owner, you know that in order to learn how to make decisions, you have to actually make them, and then once you make them, you have to make them work. Or you fail and learn the lesson you need to learn from the mistake. This is all part of the process of learning to lead an organization.

It turns out that though Bruce did handicap his son with his management style, Art eventually found his own way to run the cattle operations, but only after Bruce died. While his father was alive, Art was unable to shake off the negative and bitter attitude that he developed while working under Bruce. And it remained a burden to him even after Bruce's death.

Bruce and Art's story reminds me that it is vital to build your own family legacy from the bottom up, with positive encouragement and mentoring. If you will not build your family legacy even as you build your financial legacy, you will build a castle that will be empty of laughter, joy, and peace.

As you build your management team, I would encourage you to build a team of positive people. Choose those that are givers in every area of their lives. These are people that give you energy and are thankful and grateful to be part of the team. These are the people into whom you can pour your life, wisdom, expertise, and vision.

To build a winning management team, you will need to include people with a variety of skills. Imagine your business as a football team. Having a star quarterback is awesome, but without a strong supporting cast, that player will never live up to his potential, and you will never win a game. Just like in sports, business is about teamwork. You cannot win the exit game on your own. Surrounding yourself with a team of complementary skills different than your own is the recipe for success, and a prerequisite for a satisfying exit.

Let's say for a moment that you do have a great management team. They are reliable, highly motivated, well compensated (in your opinion) and run like a well-oiled machine. How long do you think they will last? The more successful and talented your management team is, the higher the chance someone else will try to poach them. As you plan for your transition, you need to incentivize the key employees to stay past your exit.

You do not want key employees quitting on the eve of the sale, once they find out about it. Nor do you want them to threaten to sabotage the transaction unless you pay them a nice piece of the sales price. Damage control is not planning. The plan also needs to facilitate the retention of key employees before, during, and after the transition, with agreements that predate entering into a sale process.

Years ago, we helped manage the sale of a company in the Sacramento area of California. The owner, as is typical, decided to keep the sale a secret from all the employees and customers as long as possible. That worked until the point at which the new buyer demanded the opportunity to interview key employees and a representative number of the customers.

The owner thought if he told the employees, they might try to hold him hostage by demanding part of the sale proceeds. He was also afraid the rumor mill would get started and his customers might begin to leave, reducing the value of the business. Those are real world risks, especially in industries where everyone knows the players and even more when the industry is limited to a fairly small geographic area.

In hindsight, I think he would have been better off to put in place stay bonuses for a few of the key employees in advance. That would have kept them in place in the event of a sale or his death or disability, and would remove the risk that they might attempt to extract money from him during the sale. It also tends to make the key people feel more highly valued when you bring them in and make them see that you have protected their jobs and provided them a bonus for helping out during a sale or transition. That tends to be the best way to mitigate those risks.

Having key employees that are properly incentivized also protects the company in case of the death of the owner. The only time worse for key employees to leave than during a sale, is in the event of an owner's death.

> **All the hard work of the family over many years would be lost as the value of the company plunges and employees abandon ship.**

You do not want key employees running from the company at that time, because the company will likely fail if they do. All the hard work of the family over many years would be lost as the value of the company plunges and employees abandon ship. Having key employees stay a few years past the death of the owner will give the family time to transition or decide to keep the company and move forward.

The main ways I like to incentivize key employees to stay are the following:

- Stock incentive plans

- Stay bonuses

- Deferred compensation

- Employee recognition plans

- Personal development or growth opportunities

Any employee incentive plan you undertake needs to accomplish three results. It needs to motivate, retain, and reward employees. The plan needs to motivate employees to increase the company's cash flow during the crucial phases before, during, and even after the transition process. This is usually accomplished by tying their compensation to measurable metrics such as growth numbers or profitability ratios.

Stock incentive plans provide actual equity or "phantom equity" to key employees so that they are rewarded as the value of the stock in the company rises. This can be accomplished through granting stock or stock options, or stock may be made available for purchase by employees at an advantageous price. Phantom stock plans and stock appreciation rights (SARs) are two kinds of stock plans that do not actually use any stock, but reward employees by tying compensation to the company's stock performance.

Putting in place a **stay bonus plan** for key employees to incentivize them to stay in the event of a sale or your death can be very valuable to the business. The last thing you need during your transition is disgruntled employees who feel entitled to a piece of the pie because they helped you build the business from the ground up.

If you have employees who took substantial risks with you, who stuck with you during hard times, and who have remained loyal through years of effort, they should be rewarded. As the Bible says, "A worker is worthy of his wages." On the other hand, you don't want to give away the farm. Over-rewarding employees may give them the opposite incentive than you planned. You want to compensate your employees, but not with a reward that is so large and immediate that they have no incentive to continue working with the new owner.

One of the best ways to ensure the longevity of key employees is by providing **non-qualified deferred compensation**. Deferred compensation is simply a written agreement between employer and employee in which a portion of an employee's income is paid out at a later date than it was actually earned. The owner generally gives the deferred portion in addition to current compensation, but the employee will receive it later (typically in retirement), assuming they meet the terms of the agreement, which may include a vesting schedule.

The plan is called "nonqualified" because it doesn't have the formal funding, reporting, discrimination, and employee coverage requirements of a qualified plan, and thus does not receive the same tax benefits. The best deferred compensation programs:

- Offer substantial and attractive financial benefits

- Have specific methods of attaining financial reward for key employees

- Increase the value of the company as the key employee attains his financial rewards

- Lock your key employee to the company with "golden handcuffs" (these are vesting benefits)

- Have meaningful and realistic objectives

- Are communicated effectively

Employee recognition plans are a big deal. I cannot stress enough the need to include an employee recognition plan for all of your employees. This subject could by itself be a whole book. Actually, it already is. My brother David Long recently wrote *Built to Lead: 7 Management R.E.W.A.R.D.S Principles for Becoming a Top 10 percent Manager*, named as a Top Ten Book by the Wall Street Journal. It is written to help you lead. It provides a step-by-step approach to driving your management to a new level. As you drive everyone else, they attain new heights as well.

The book is well worth the read, and the information in it is integral to building a company that eventually does not need you to run it.

Some employees are motivated to stay with a company because they see that a company spends time and money on personal development of their employees, which is very important to them. Others join a company and stay because they see that the company is on a growth curve of which they want to be part—especially if they are granted stock options!

In April, 2011, we were brought in by a CPA firm in the Tampa, Florida area to help a fairly large business client create an exit plan for the owner, and to provide wealth management services for his family. One of the issues we spotted during our planning was a bloated profit sharing plan for an older management team, with no goals or metrics to meet in order to participate. After input from the CPA firm, we recommended they scrap that plan and start over.

It was replaced with a bonus system for the management team in which they all shared in the bonus pool created by reaching a certain level of revenue and then added another level in which management of each department could receive an extra bonus if they met certain metrics unique to their departments. Finally, we proposed a deferred compensation for the key employees, as designated by the owners, which paid a ten-year income benefit at age sixty-five. The deferred compensation became part of the compensation plan for the new management team we were building. Now we had a management team aligned with the owners' goals of growing the company!

In order to motivate, retain, and reward your employees, you will need to create a sound and thoughtful incentive plan that provides an earmarked and significant slice of the future value of the business to the key employees who helped create that same value. Depending on the circumstances of how you grew your business, your management team may expect its share of the windfall you receive from the sale. The BraveHeart Planning Process™ prepares for this expectation by implementing incentive plans with golden handcuffs. That way everyone is pulling together at the time of sale or transition due to the death of an owner.

"Golden handcuffs" tie the key employees to the business through the use of deferred benefits. You give employees the rights to certain rewards, but vest the rewards so that the employees can only realize their full reward by continuing to work for the company during the transition process and through any earn-out period imposed by a buyer during a sale. Finally, it is vital that the incentive plan be perceived as a win-win situation for both the company and the key employees.

Most importantly, you need to hire qualified, highly motivated and high performing workers. Providing opportunities for personal development or growth opportunities within the company can help keep them engaged and excited about coming to work. In order to keep this kind of worker, they need to know they are highly valued. Even an acknowledgment on a regular basis of their small successes within the company can go a long way. Appreciate them and they will do a better job for you. Those people are the kind that have a high degree of care for the customers and desire to build a business along with you.

Operating Systems

The next VC is having a company with strong operating systems. Paula Cope, a business consultant,[23] defines a system as a group of related processes that generate recurring revenue from an established and growing customer base or create financial efficiencies. These systems can range from core processes that control expenses such as production or service delivery, to people-related processes such as succession planning or a performance management approach. It is important to not only make sure your business has these systems, but also that they are well-documented and highly efficient.

Diversified Customer/Supplier Base

The next most important VC after systems is a diversified customer and supplier base. Think like a buyer for a moment: If you had the choice to buy two identical businesses except that one had fifty customers and the other had two customers, which would you choose? I think we'd all prefer the one with fifty customers.

Remember the discussion we had on risk? Just like an investment in stocks, diversification of customers lowers risk. If you only have a few customers, you are exposing buyers to the very real risk of one of those customers leaving with you. Even if a buyer is willing to purchase your business with limited customers, he will probably structure the deal to include significant earn outs or holdbacks to minimize that risk. All things being equal, a buyer would likely pay a significantly higher price for the business with many customers.

Same thing applies to more than one supplier. If you are totally dependent on one supplier, they can hold you hostage or take you down with them if they go under. If they are unable to get raw materials due to weather issues or political risk somewhere in the world, you get cut off from your supply. Only bad things can come from having one supplier.

Recurring Revenue

Recurring revenue, after the management team, is the most important of the VC's in my opinion. A company that has recurring revenue does not have to start over every year in wondering how it will do. It has a built in cashflow machine that gives it an advantage over other businesses. Every year it builds upon all of the previous years' work to build the company and this puts it on a very nice growth curve, which as we discuss later, is very important to buyers. A buyer will see a company like this as a lower risk purchase and it will greatly aid in convincing a buyer to consider your business when you are ready to exit.

Realistic Growth Strategy

Have you ever pitched your company to a group of venture capital investors? Whether you have or not, it is helpful to steal a page from the VC playbook when selling your established business. If you have ever seen one of these presentations conducted, you know that buyers pay a premium for realistic growth strategies. Realism is of vital interest in a VC environment, but it is also extremely important when selling a traditional business.

After all, what buyers really pay for is a growing, future cash flow. The more convincingly you can show them that your business will generate that for them, the more they will pay.

Your growth strategy needs to be communicated to potential buyers in such a way that they see actual, concrete reasons that cash flow will grow after they acquire your business. After all, what buyers really pay for is a growing, future cash flow. The more convincingly you can show them that your business will generate that for them, the more they will pay.

Buyers will not understand your business as well as you, so they will miss opportunities that you see. Sometimes they will pointedly ignore opportunities they see in order to suppress their asking price. It is your job, and the job of your representatives, to present opportunities convincingly in a written growth plan. As important as it is that your business operation needs to be sustainable without your involvement, it is also important that your growth plan can function without your participation. Build a strategic growth plan that does not depend upon you.

Financial Controls

The existence of reliable financial controls is a VC often overlooked. Financial controls are used to manage the business. Documented controls not only safeguard the company's assets, but are also an invaluable tool for management. If your business is an acquisition target by a third party, the potential buyer will comb through your financials with a very fine toothed comb. If the buyer is not totally and completely comfortable with the numbers, he will give you a lowball offer or call the whole thing off. Buyers know that numbers do the real talking. The more confidence they have in your numbers, the more cash they will fork over. The sooner you implement these, the better the control you will have in your business as it grows and the more you can rely on them for decision making.

Proprietary Technology

According to Kevin Short, author of *Sell Your Business for an Outrageous Price*, "Owning a company in a business sector that the market considers "hot" certainly never hurts value. The problem is predicting what will be hot when you are ready to sell." Since it is nearly impossible to position your company in an attractive sector—you are pretty much stuck in whatever industry you are in—it is more important to develop protected systems and proprietary technology. Control of proprietary technology can make the value of a business far greater than the capitalization of historical earnings.

My friend, John Brown, an attorney I consider to be the father of exit planning, tells of one client named Will Rogers in his book *Cash Out and Move On,* who quadrupled the value of his business based on the development of proprietary technology alone.[24]

According to John,

> Will owned a small systems engineering firm that designed and installed cellular networks. Like many small service businesses, Will's company had a sporadic earnings history. The most recent three years' profit and cash flow had been declining and Will had been told by his CPA that the business did not have much value.
>
> On the surface, I would have agreed with Will's CPA. When I probed further, however, and asked why the company had lost money in the past three years, I learned that Will had been investing heavily in the research and development of a new switching device. This device could revolutionize cellular and wireless switching networks technology and was particularly applicable in the development of wireless networks, which were just beginning to emerge. Through further inquiry, I learned that this technology was patentable and that Will was certain that it would greatly enhance the services his company could provide. Supporting Will's assertion was a multi-million dollar contract from an international wireless communication technology.

Will's story illustrates the fact that sometimes buyers are more interested in your proprietary protected technology for its potential to augment their own business ventures than they are in your business. You may be able to sell off a protected technology by itself for cash, and still keep your business!

Growing Cash Flow

The bottom line in creating VCs is quite literally the bottom line. Ultimately all VCs are designed to contribute to the stability and growth of cash flow. Cash flow is the key metric in buyer purchasing equations. Buyers don't generally buy your business for its equipment, its facilities, its appearance, or its goodwill; they buy for cash flow. They will pay top dollar for cash flow that they believe will increase after they make an acquisition.

Suppose you had two companies. One company made $2 million for three years in a row. The other company made $1 million the first year, $2 million the second year, and $3 million the third year. Which company would you buy? Even though the overall total cash flows are the same, you would want the second company. Why? Buyers pay for growth. Any company that is not growing is dying. Growth is the lifeblood of a company. That is why it is so important that cash flow be substantial and increasing for the years just prior to the sale. Buyers are willing to pay more for companies with increasing cash flows.

Value catalysts are a vital portion of the BraveHeart Planning Process™. They preserve value and reduce the risks associated with owning a business. They also enhance the prospect that the business will grow significantly in the next few years. Whether you are planning on transitioning to an insider or an outsider, it is important to work on VCs. In the event of an inside transfer, VCs must be in place so that the business will continue to generate the income stream the owner will need to be paid out in order to step aside and/or retire. In the event of a sale, the business will need VCs to attract buyers willing to pay top dollar.

Avoiding Reliance on 1-2 Key Sales People or Product Design People

It is not rocket science for me to suggest that if your business is built on one or two key sales people or product design people, a buyer will not likely pay top dollar for it. This makes you vulnerable to your employees as a business owner and also introduces risk in a buyer's mind when they are considering buying your company. If you do have this kind of situation, you had better consider tying them down to your company with some kind of incentive plan that acts a pair of golden handcuffs as we mentioned above.

Family Value Catalysts

The steps surrounding familial growth will encompass different aspects than the business side, but the strategy is surprisingly similar. Families with generational wealth often look much like a business, with a constitution, family council, and sometimes even a family bank.

Though we will spend a good amount of time on the structures of a successful family in the financial realm, we must remember that, as our good friends at the Bonner Family Office write, "The real wealth of a family is not financial. The primary assets are the family members and their unique talents, knowledge and experience. After all, if you pass along significant financial wealth without the means to manage it, it will be more of a curse than a blessing, and your family will not possess that money for long."[25]

The catalysts for creating family value (what we call "legacy") may include:

- Estate Plan

- Family Limited Partnerships/Limited Liability Company

- Education Plans

- Donor Advised Fund

- Dynasty Trust

- Annual Gifting Plan

The Estate Plan

Estate planning is the very first step in catalyzing value for your family. Just like VCs in business, estate planning and the rest are designed to help you transfer assets to the next generation, protecting your core interests, and increasing the impact of your organization. Estate planning specifically will ensure your care if you become incompetent, the care of your family, the distribution of your property, and the minimization of tax.

> **If you fail to plan, the government has a plan for you.**

Basic estate planning starts with creating a living trust and a will. Using a living trust is the private method by which you can control your assets during your life and at death. We use these for almost all of our clients. The will is a legal document that clearly states who will take care of your minor children and, if you have no living trust, who will receive your assets. Dying without a will or a trust ensures that the state will control the distribution of your estate. If you fail to plan, they have a plan for you of their own making.

The second most important estate planning documents are advance directives, such as a durable power of attorney, a medical power of attorney, and a living will. These documents enable you to appoint agents to act on your behalf should you become incompetent or unable to manage your own affairs.

Family Limited Partnerships/Limited Liability Company's

For families whose wealth is growing and who wish to control risk, family limited partnerships (FLPs) or limited liability companies (LLCs) are essential VCs.

In family limited partnerships (FLPs), at least one of the owners is considered a "general" partner who makes business decisions and is personally liable for business debts. But FLPs also have at least one "limited" partner who invests money in the business but has minimal control over daily business decisions and operations. The advantage for these limited partners is that they are not personally liable for business debts. They have the pass-through taxation of a partnership.

FLPs are incredibly beneficial instruments, if they are structured correctly. They may allow a family to reduce or eliminate estate taxes, secure assets in a single entity, give parents full control of their family legacy, keep assets in the family, simplify gifting, and provide protection from creditors and litigators.

LLCs are similar in that it is a business structure that combines the pass-through taxation of a partnership or sole proprietorship, with the limited liability of a corporation. They seem simple to the uninformed, but can be quite complex.

It is imperative that you consult with a competent attorney when setting up an FLP or LLC. In order for the entity to work the way in which it was designed, it needs to be run completely by the book. That means you will need to comply with state law filings, write up a partnership agreement, open a bank account, file tax returns, keep records immaculately, and comply with a host of other guidelines. Your business or estate planning attorney should guide you through the complex rules of FLP or LLC creation and maintenance.

Education Plan

Most of our clients' children do not qualify for federal or state aid because the parents earn too much money. So we will discuss a few options for setting aside funds for college.

It is more imperative than ever to diligently plan for your children's education. College costs have exploded in the last thirty years. Between 1950 and 1970, sending a kid to a public university cost about four percent of an American family's annual income. Forty years later, in 2010, it accounted for an astounding 11 percent. Moody's released statistics showing tuition and fees rising 300 percent vs. the Consumer Price Index between 1990 and 2011.[26] There are plenty of tools that can help you, including 529 plans, irrevocable trusts, and Uniform Gifts to Minors, also known as UGMAs (or Uniform Transfer to Minors, depending on the state you live in).

- *529 Plan*

A 529 Plan is a tax-deferred, state-sponsored tuition plan that can come in one of two forms: savings or prepaid tuition. In a savings plan, parents or grandparents can contribute cash to an account to pay for a child's future higher education expenses. The donor selects from the plan's investment options, usually mutual funds, to grow the account. Most states offer 529 savings plans. You can choose any state plan to create your 529, without restrictions.

One of the unique features of a 529 plan is that there are no income limits in order to qualify. Depending on a particular state's plans, individuals can contribute until the 529 savings plan account reaches between $200,000 and $300,000 through investments or growth. Plus the owner of the plan can choose between investment options, though these are limited in number. Investment strategies can be changed once a year or when a beneficiary is changed.

Being able to change beneficiaries is another feature of the 529 that is not common to most education funding vehicles. The beneficiary on the account can be changed as often as desired, but in order to have a non-taxable and penalty-free change, the new beneficiary must be a member of the family of the prior beneficiary. The plan also allows participants to roll over amounts tax-free from one plan to another as often as once every twelve months, without the need to change beneficiaries. While contributions to qualified state tuition programs such as the 529 are not tax deductible, the investments do grow tax-free.

A 529 Pre-paid Tuition Plan, on the other hand, allows parents to lock in today's tuition costs for the future by purchasing units today that are redeemable at US colleges or universities. If the cost of college goes up in the future, the pre-paid units are guaranteed to pay for tuition and fees for in-state public schools at the current price. These prepaid units may be transferable to private colleges or out-of-state universities. The Independent 529 plan is available for more than 300 private colleges for future tuition discounts.

- *Irrevocable Trusts*

Anyone contemplating giving a large gift to a minor will quickly run into difficulties. Aside from the practical problems associated with a minor's legal incapacity to enter into contracts and other agreements, there is the issue of responsibility. Because minors have no legal capacity to open accounts on their own, gifts to minors are often made under the shelter of a trust, which provides a trustee to aid in the prudent management of the money. For education planning purposes, many people establish a custodial trust for their children. Custodial trusts come in two flavors: the 2503(b) and the 2503(c) trust.

A 2503(b) is an irrevocable trust set up for the benefit of a minor. It can hold any type of property and can have more than one beneficiary. One of the downsides to this trust is that all income from the trust must be distributed to the beneficiary annually. However, the corpus of the trust does not have to be distributed to the beneficiary at twenty-one. In fact, the corpus can be held for as long as the beneficiary lives. Also, the entire amount placed into the trust can be counted as a present interest gift, which qualifies for the annual gift exclusion.

A 2503(c) is very similar to the 2503(b) except for a few key differences, namely that only one trust beneficiary is permitted, the trust does not require the trustee to distribute income currently, and the trust requires the distribution of accumulated income and principal when the minor reaches the age of twenty-one. One way to provide continued management of the trust past age twenty-one is to give the child a brief window of opportunity to take control of trust assets when he turns twenty-one. If he waives this right, the assets can remain in the trust for as long as the donor provided when he established the trust.

- *UGMA/UTMA*

Gifts to minors may be deposited into custodial accounts to save for a child's education or other future needs. A custodial account is like a trust, except that the terms are set in the state statute rather than in a trust document. In a custodian account, the contributor or donor (grantor) gives an irrevocable gift to a minor (beneficiary). The custodian controls the account for the benefit of the child while the child is a minor. The custodian must comply with the particular state's UGMA/UTMA statute. Upon reaching the age of majority (age eighteen, twenty-one, or twenty-five, depending on state), the child will assume control of the account. There is only one custodian and one minor allowed per property held as gift to minor.[27]

Two drawbacks are:

1. When the minor reaches the state's age of majority, the property comes under the control of the beneficiary. Neither the donor nor the custodian can place any conditions on those funds once the minor reaches this age. Therefore, even if the donor was hoping that the minor would use the money for education, he or she can choose to use it any way he or she wishes. Financial aid can also be less for a college applicant who has assets held as a UGMA or UTMA.

2. Many funding options have income level phase-outs so many higher income earners turn to UGMAs or UTMAs (depending

on the state). UTMAs are a tad more flexible, but the two acts are very similar. One big difference, however, is that UGMAs terminate when the child reaches age eighteen, while UTMAs terminate at twenty-one. The Uniform Gift to Minors Act (or alternately the Uniform Transfer to Minors Act) provides a simple way for assets to be held by/for minors. UGMAs allow minors to hold securities, though not the right to apply for a brokerage account.

Two benefits of gift to minor ownership are:

1. They are much less complicated and less expensive than creating a trust with the minor as the beneficiary.

2. A portion of the income from interest, capital gains, and dividends is taxed at the child's tax rate once they reach age fourteen, which is typically lower than that of the parents.

Taking charge of your family's education is vital in today's increasingly competitive world and UGMAs are just one strategy to implement. With modern technology, your children can have an education designed for them. They can begin to focus on some special niche early on in their education because specialists in almost any field make more money. You must take ownership of your children's education. It is not the school system's job to raise or educate your children. It is up to you to teach them how to become men and women of creativity, manners, and diligence.

Donor Advised Fund

I often recommend Donor Advised Funds (DAFs), and have one myself. They are very flexible, simple and cheap to administer. According to the National Philanthropic Trust, a DAF is a philanthropic vehicle established at a public charity. DAFs allow donors to receive an immediate tax benefit when they place the assets into the fund, which they can direct to charities according to their prerogative. The National Philanthropic Trust analogizes Donor-advised Funds to a charitable savings account: a donor contributes as frequently to the fund as he would like and then recommends grants to the charity of his choice when he is ready.

DAFs have a number of characteristics that include:

- Contributions of personal assets are irrevocable

- Immediate reception of the maximum tax deduction allowed by the IRS

- Ability to name the fund account, advisors, and any successors or charitable beneficiaries

- Assets in the fund can be invested and grow tax-free

The first DAFs were created in the '30s, but they didn't receive a legal structure from Congress until 1969. By the 90s they began to receive attention and in recent years, the number and popularity of DAFs has increased rapidly. Grants from DAFs reached nearly $10 billion in 2013 while contributions to DAFs total more than 5 percent of all charitable giving in the US. Assets held within DAFs total more than $50 billion.[28]

I like DAFs for the $5-$50 million net worth client range, especially because they allow the donor a great deal of control. DAFs are a flexible and efficient way to set up a charitable organization, particularly because they are much easier to create than a private foundation. Another bonus is that they can be hosted by the same companies that hold your investment assets (Schwab, Fidelity, Vanguard, etc.) or community foundations.

Dynasty Trust

Dynasty trusts are a foundational structure for families who desire to leave financial legacies. They can greatly reduce your family's future estate tax bill, allow you to adopt an endowment model for your family, and help you to maintain your long-term investment horizon. Dynasty trusts function much like an ordinary trust in many ways. They require a written agreement and appointment of a trustee to manage property and administer the trust according to the terms of the trust agreement.

What makes dynasty trusts attractive is that they let you retain much longer control over your assets than other trust models. Dynasty trusts are irrevocable, meaning the assets held by the trust are removed from your taxable estate. They are also designed to be perpetual, staying in place for the long-term growth of your family fortune. Dynasty trusts can also be designed to be free from transfer taxes.

The dynasty trust can be used as a vehicle to help you create a family council. Family councils are a vital dynamic of a Legacy Family, which we will talk about in a later chapter. The dynasty trust can spell out who serves on the family council and how they are appointed. The family council in turn, gets to decide when to distribute funds to the beneficiaries of the trust.[29]

Annual Gifting Plan

You can use your annual exclusion gifts of $14,000 (for 2015) per person to fund a number of possible entities for use in your Education Plan for college funding. That plan can include irrevocable trusts, 529 plans, or UTMA/UGMA accounts.

Value is not built in a day. **Step 4: Value Catalysts**, is perhaps the longest step in the BraveHeart Planning Process™. Building VCs will create value in your business for yourself, not just your successor. The strategies discussed in this chapter are worth implementing even if the rest of the process is completely ignored. Creating a business of value and a family of legacy is more than just an exit strategy; it's a life-changing process that could alter the whole course of your life and the life of your family for generations.

CHAPTER 6

Business Durability

Rome, Italy, 753 B.C.–1453 A.D.

The Roman Empire was brutal. Enslaving thousands and leaving the slain in his wake, each new emperor relentlessly set off to conquer new lands. Civilization after civilization fell to its might. At its height, the Roman Empire was the largest political and social structure in the Western world. Rome wasn't impressive just for its breadth, however, but also for its durability. At Caesar Augustus's death, he proclaimed that he had "found Rome a city of clay, but left it a city of marble." The Pax Romana, *or the "Peace of Rome," ushered in a time of peace and prosperity for a thousand years.*

Rome's legacy is legendary, not only for her military prowess, but also for her inventions and innovations. The ancient world was transformed, as technological advancements were spread throughout the Roman Empire. Fifty thousand miles of road connected scientists and artisans, architects and philosophers. Ideas flowed seamlessly, and improvements were developed in the fields of medicine, religion, government, and law.

Her rule was ordered and efficient. She had four classes of people, a division near and dear to the Roman citizen. Every man knew his place, and each performed his role for the good of the whole, as one together, E Pluribus Unum, "out of many, one." In battle, when one man fell, another would take his place, the line never wavering, the shield formation never broken. Every move made with purpose.

Instead of subjecting conquered lands to mere slavery, Rome enveloped them into the Roman culture. She allowed inclusion for every tribe, as long as they paid allegiance to the crown. In return, she gave all a government that represented the citizen voice, the Senatus Populus, *or "Senate and People of Rome." She ruled with a stern hand, but made it possible for many to achieve a life of which they would have never dreamed.*

In the end, Rome was built to endure. Fading away was never an option. From their military prowess to their quick-drying cement, Rome was established on the idea that Rome would never end. All Romans were born with one belief, one goal in mind: to create an Empire that would last through the ages. Anything less was less than Roman.

Rome, for all of its flaws, was built brick by brick to endure. Our American culture lacks that endurance. We are a young people, but already we gravitate to the individual, the carefree, the fleeting, and the moment. One of my least favorite corporate slogans is Pepsi's "Live for Now." Our entire society is devoted to instant gratification. You hear it on the radio, you see it on the television, and you witness it in the people all around you. Americans want it all and they want it now.

Whether you like it or not, your family business is in a culture war. Society preaches prosperity of the moment, but your business needs investment for the future, and your family needs you to sacrifice for them. Corporate culture teaches you to climb the ladder, but your family business needs you to man the helm. You must not succumb to culture's campaign against longevity.

You cannot accept defeat in your business.

You cannot accept defeat in your business. You must live to fight another day, or there is no growth, no jobs, and no retirement. You have to be able to survive the many hard and uncomfortable challenges you will face to reap the ultimate benefits and to provide for your family and your employees. Owning a business is no walk in the park. It is not an easy arena in which to play. The vast majority of businesses fail. It takes a BraveHeart to carry on. It takes a business with durability to last.

Longevity, not just short-term profitability, is the goal of The BraveHeart Planning Process™. **Step 5: Durability** is devoted to creating a business that could last for generations. Think of the ancestral homes of the feudal days. Those castles have lasted through thousands of years of wars, hurricanes, wildfires, and national emergencies. Just as a clan would take refuge in a castle in times of trouble, so too can a Legacy Family rely on a durable business to survive through lean times.

Business durability and continuity face two key challenges: the loss of an owner and the loss of the company's key talent. We will also delve into a few other risks to the business and family on the financial side as well as dive into a discussion of the mitigation of those risks, but the biggest risk to your business is yourself. Would your business be able to survive without you? No one likes to talk about death, including entrepreneurs, but it is an important discussion to have. Your business and your family need to be ready in case disaster strikes.

As an entrepreneur myself, I know that in order to be successful in business you have to have vision and optimism. No one succeeds at business believing he will fail, and consequently owners, above most other people, hate to think about their own passing. This unbounded optimism is an entrepreneur's greatest strength, but it can also turn into his Achilles heel. Aristotle called a hero's fatal flaw Hamartia, meaning to fail or miss the mark.[30] In Greek tragedies, the source

> This unbounded optimism is an entrepreneur's greatest strength, but it can also become his Achilles heel.

of a hero's greatest strength was also his greatest weakness. Optimism is usually a good thing, but left unchecked by realism, it can make owners avoid planning for anything other than the most optimistic outcome. This leaves the company and the family in deep trouble when bad things happen.

Whether you engage in the rest of the process or not, you must make sure your business can survive your death, disability, or retirement, as well as making sure it can endure the loss of the company's key talent.

If you were to leave suddenly, would your management team be equipped to carry on without your guidance, reputation, and expertise? Does everything that happens in the business have to pass through you, or can the business operate without you? What about the company's financing? If you have personally secured any loans, will those loans be called upon your death?

If you have personally guaranteed any equipment or real property leases, it is unlikely these will be renewed. If your business relies on bonding capability to run, it will probably dry up unless someone other than you holds the professional credentials or capital necessary for the bonding. If you have taken out personal loans in your own name, your creditors may come calling. Only God knows the day of your death. As unfortunate as it is, your family and the business both need to be prepared for this contingency.

What about your ownership interest? Do you have a buy-sell agreement in place to buyout deceased partners, due to an untimely death?

Your disability is another risk to your organization and your family. Have you cross-trained your employees? Do you have a management team in place that can operate without you? Have you powers of attorney to protect the family and the business? Without the needed documentation, your family will have to swim through a morass of bureaucracy and have to get court approval to make necessary decisions. You may not be worried about what will happen to your business and family should you be disabled, but you should be, if only because you love your family. Prepare for disability by making sure you have powers of attorney signed and have adequate insurance coverage.

Suppose everything goes exactly to plan and you avoid both death and disability. Either way, your day of retirement is still approaching. Regardless of whether you decide to transition the business to a child or decide to keep your ownership, you will still need to make sure you have set aside adequate assets for your retirement income. I like to see our clients diversify out of the need for income from the company by the time they retire. One never knows how the business will do once you leave. The economy could tank or the business could be dealt a blow. Your business may suffer some loss that will cause it to fail. S&P 500-sized companies still fail from time to time.

Even if your company continues to run like clockwork, preparing ahead of time for retirement is still a wise decision. Depending on how things go, the business may not have the cash flow needed to pay you until you die. Your successor might struggle to pay the employees needed to replace you or he may have to live in near poverty just to keep things afloat so you can get paid. Waiting till retirement is not a smart plan. Relying solely on the business to pay you throughout your retirement is a risky gambit. You need to plan for and fund your retirement before you hit transition time.

The second key challenge is making sure your business can survive the loss of the company's key talent. Who does the company rely on to bring in new business, maintain key relationships, or oversee critical operations? How have you prepared for the loss of key talent? Would your employees and customers remain if your key talent left?

Have you considered what needs to be done to hedge the risk of losing key talent upon which the company depends?

We took on a case on the East Coast a few years ago. The mission was to help the family build a new management team to transition control of their company to the son. It is very common to find a management team roughly the same age as the one who is running the company. If you are not careful, you can end up with an exodus of people who want to retire with the owner. You need to look forward, as did our client, to foresee that problem and solve it, before it threatens your company.

Business Durability Structures

Four key structures are often necessary to manage a business transition in the case of a tragic accident, disability, or even a normal retirement scenario.

- Buy/Sell Agreements

- Deferred Compensation

- Key Employee Insurance

- Legal Audit

The theater mantra applies perfectly. Regardless of what happens, "the show must go on." The heart of the BraveHeart Planning Process™ is the goal of building something that is bigger than you, something that can outlast you for the benefit of the business and the family.

My favorite story of both family legacy and business continuity is the Beretta Corporation. If you are unfamiliar with firearms, Beretta is a world famous Italian small arms manufacturer. Their weapons are used by law enforcement, military, and private citizens the world over. While you have probably heard of their products, you may not know that the company itself has been continuously in business since the early 16th century.[31] Not only that, but the business has been owned by the same family throughout its history. Beretta's succession plan is simple but elegant. In every new generation, a select few company officers are groomed for key business positions from the family's ranks, but everyone gets a share of the company stock. As the family has grown, so have the company's profits. Thus, though each successive heir gets a smaller and smaller share of the total wealth, they have continued to grow a bigger and bigger fortune.

If your goal is to have wealth sustained through generations, you could not do much better than to emulate the Beretta family. To do this, you will need to make sure the business can survive without you. It won't last two generations, much less dozens, if it is built solely around your own skills. Now your goal may not be to transfer to family members once you retire, but even if you are looking to sell, continuity is a vital ingredient of the process. Remember what we've discussed about risk-averse buyers? The more risk variables you can eliminate, the more valuable the company will be.

Buy/Sell Agreement

For businesses with more than a single owner, we cannot overemphasize the importance of the buy/sell agreement (or as it is formally known: the business continuity agreement). It is one of the most important documents of your career. It ensures the proper execution of your wishes should you need to exit the business under less than favorable circumstances.

The buy/sell agreement is the definitive document that controls the transfer of ownership between owners in certain key situations. These usually include your death or incapacitation. More robust agreements also contain agreements to transfer ownership in the event of an owner's permanent and total disability, termination of employment, retirement, bankruptcy, divorce, or a business dispute among the owners.

I am astounded at the number of businesses that do not have this basic agreement in place. Some years ago, I was brought in to help solve a problem created by the death of one of four brothers that owned a large contracting company together. There was no buy/sell agreement in place that would enable the survivors to buy out the deceased brother's spouse. We finally resolved the issues, but not before she extracted a significant amount of money and emotion from the boys and the business. That was one painful lesson for all parties involved.

A buy/sell agreement is a legally enforceable contract. It is most often used to give co-owners the right of first refusal if you are planning on selling your stake of the business. It can also be designed to compel co-owners to buy your stock should you no longer be able to participate materially in the business. The terms vary among different agreements, but the purpose remains the same: to protect the business and the interest of the owners should something bad happen to one of them. The remaining owners get the security of knowing that an outsider (such as the family that inherits your ownership or the third party to whom your family sells) will not be able to make decisions and the deceased or incapacitated owner gets the assurance that his family will be bought out for a reasonable price.

In order to assure a reasonable price, it is vital that the buy/sell agreement establishes the value of the stock, gives additional protection to all the owners, and sets the terms and conditions of the buyout. For your buy/sell agreement to do its job properly, it needs to explain to whom the owners can sell, at what price and terms, and under what restrictions. A buy/sell agreement has a number of advantages. It will ensure that ownership in the business can only be transferred by the methods and terms set out by the agreement.

A buy/sell agreement establishes and protects the rights of shareholders, as well as fixing the interest rate, length of buyout period, and security of any transfer of stock. A buy/sell agreement is the key continuity document of privately held businesses. If you have co-owners and no buy/sell agreement, it should be your top priority to have one drafted as soon as possible by a business attorney who has handled many business sales.

The buy/sell agreement may call for the company to buy the shares or for the other owners to buy the shares. There are pros and cons for each of those options. You will want to investigate the options as you consult with your business attorney.

Also, buy/sell agreements can be funded or unfunded. To the extent it is funded, it is typically accomplished with insurance. If unfunded, there is generally a small down payment and then payments over a number of years. We prefer to have the agreements funded as much as possible to make sure the deceased's family realizes the funds they need to take care of themselves.

Deferred Compensation

We talked about deferred compensation at some length in our last chapter on value catalysts, so I will not cover the same ground here. In this chapter, we are going to take a look at deferred compensation from a business continuity and risk management perspective, rather than from a value maximization perspective. Having key employees invested in the company goes a long way when calamity strikes.

Remember, deferred compensation is simply a written agreement between employer and employee in which a portion of an employee's income is paid out at a later date than it was actually earned. The owner generally gives the deferred portion in addition to current compensation, but the employee will receive it later (typically in retirement), assuming they meet the terms of the agreement, which may include a vesting schedule. A vesting schedule is designed to have you qualify for the agreed deferred compensation amount over time, as an inducement to keep the employee long-term.

If you do not have the timeframe to implement a full deferred compensation program, you may want to look into a stay bonus plan. A stay bonus plan consists of a written, funded plan to provide monthly or quarterly bonuses over a twelve to eighteen-month period for key employees to remain with the company during the transition to a new owner, due to a sale or death of an owner. Stay bonuses are very effective for a third party transfer, but they also apply to insider transfers as well. You wouldn't want your employees to quit on your children or successor any more than you would want them to run out on a buyer. In fact, it may be even more important to have sustainable management if your designated successor is young and you are depending on continued cash flow from the business.

Key Employee Insurance

The last component to a durable company is key employee insurance. Of all situations, the one that is likely to have the most impact on your bottom line, as well as the very survival of your business, is the loss of one key employee or a group of employees. Should you lose a key person to an unplanned retirement, resignation, death, or disability, your company will suffer, unless you are prepared. When the success of the entire firm depends on a small group of people, it is vital that your exit planner first identifies these people and then implements a plan to minimize the risk of their loss.

Usually risk mitigation involves taking out a life insurance policy (owned by the business) on each of the key employees. The business pays the premiums and receives the death benefits. When determining how much life insurance to purchase, it is important to develop an estimate of where from, at what cost, and how quickly a replacement can be hired and trained, because the proceeds of the insurance policy will be used to recruit and train a replacement employee, as well as cover the income lost from the employee's untimely exit. Determining the cost of a replacement will help the firm determine its exposure to loss. Having suitable replacements already positioned inside the firm can substantially mitigate this risk.

In a small business, the only key employee may be the owner. If that is the case, the loss of your own drive, experience, and dedication would be a crippling blow that the business would not be able to overcome. If you are the only key employee—you wake up every morning and look at the business in the mirror—it will be almost impossible to keep the company afloat even with insurance. No amount of money can replace a

> The loss of your own drive, experience, and dedication would be a crippling blow that the business would not be able to overcome.

sole practitioner, which is why I cannot stress enough how important it is that you create value in your business apart from yourself by training a group of competent managers, or at the very least, grooming a capable successor. If you are unwilling or unable to grow your business beyond yourself, then what you really have is a job, or maybe a lifestyle business, not a saleable business.

Legal Audit

Before jumping into family durability measures, I want to deal with your responsibilities under the law. My clients are mostly business owners or their spouses and children. They tend to be conservative in how they live and how they vote. They also tend to hate attorneys, and sometimes CPAs, or anyone else attached to the system that makes their lives complicated. My clients hate anyone who assists the government in taking excess taxes from them. They also hate those who would try to use the system to take from them all they have earned. The personal injury lottery is a huge part of this problem.

I live under the same system. I don't like it any more than my clients, but that does not change the facts. If you do not have competent legal and tax counsel, you are going into a tank battle with a water pistol. You must hire competent help. The law is written to benefit those who plan and to penalize those who do not plan. It is that simple. If you want to fight politically, then fight. But that does not mean you should roll over and pay more tax or take on more risk than you should.

For that reason, when I run a BraveHeart Plan, I bring in a law firm to do a legal audit of the business. Yes, I said audit. When they hear the word "audit," most people immediately think of accounting, but in its most general sense, an audit is an overview, an inspection, or examination. It is a review. The purpose of an accounting audit is to verify the accuracy of your financial records and the information contained in your statements. Most accounting audits are conducted by an independent accounting firm that verifies the statement, putting its stamp of approval on the books. A legal audit operates much the same way. It is like an accounting audit in that a lawyer will review your legal documents with the same attention to detail that a CPA would give to your books.

A legal audit puts the legal affairs of your business under a microscope. Your attorney team should walk through your existing practices, procedures, and documents to uncover potential legal problems. It begins with a review of basic corporate documents such as the articles of incorporation, bylaws, minutes of shareholder meetings and board of directors meetings, and the stock book showing all past stock transactions. From there the audit looks into operating documents such as contracts with third parties, loan documents, leases, and a whole tide of agreements regarding employment, retirement plans, trade secrecy, intellectual property and the transfer of stock, among many other things.

Finally, the lawyer will examine your ongoing practices and procedures for potential liability. A number of places to look for pitfalls include hiring and firing practices, insurance coverage, environmental issues, workers compensation, and unemployment compensation. When it comes time to sell, if you are sued, or if you suffer a legal audit by the IRS or other government entity, you will be glad you had conducted a legal audit. And, if you do sell, any M&A firm worth its salt will dive deeply into your legal documents, looking for any signs of trouble.

Family Durability

Ensuring the survival of your business is only half the battle. You must also ensure that your family is prepared to face the potential tragic effects of the risks they are exposed to every single day. When I take clients through the BraveHeart Planning Process™, I conduct a review of their entire personal risk management approach. It is important that your advisor takes a 30,000-foot view of your risk on both sides of your life so that he can see the big picture. I often find large gaps in my clients' coverage. The following section outlines some of the more common problems I find, as well as the strategies to mitigate them.

Personal Property Casualty Review

We like to obtain a property/casualty review of your business and personal affairs, usually by the same competent organization. We like property/ casualty companies to be not just a seller of insurance but also to work with us, acting as a consultant for what is needed and what is in the best interest of the client.

America is a litigious society. Our robust court system is among the most advanced in the world, but it is also bogged down by an overwhelming amount of lawsuits. Not only is the number of lawsuits large and growing, but so is the size of the settlements and jury awards. It has become a lottery system for those who would sue. The odds seem to be continuously growing in favor of those who choose to sue, regardless of the weak basis for the lawsuit.

If you are worth a few million dollars or more, you should look for firms that are able to write policies from the higher end insurance companies. Generally you can get a good guess at the level of sophistication of a broker based on the types of companies he writes from. Higher end brokers provide the type of policies our clients generally need. A few of the property/casualty companies the brokers should be able to write insurance with are ACE Group, The Chubb Group, PURE (Privilege Underwriters Reciprocal Exchange), and AIG Private Client Group.

However, regardless of who you use as a property/casualty broker, you should make it clear to them that you want them to review this for you in the capacity of a consultant, not just a salesman. Ask them this question: If you were me—and assuming you understand my risks—what insurance coverages would you buy and with what companies would you place that coverage?

It is the job of an exit planner to help you find competent counsel as needed, and that includes property/casualty brokers. I like to have input in the planning with the broker to understand my clients' overall risk profile. I also want to understand the possibility of my client being sued successfully for an amount that is considerably greater than his current liability policy limits.

What our firm almost always recommends is buying a commercial umbrella policy, which can be purchased in order to offer the following coverage:

- Excess coverage over underlying liability coverage when those policy limits are not sufficient to pay for judgments against the company

- Comprehensive coverage available for losses and exposures left completely uncovered by the underlying policies

- Drop-down coverage, which means that the umbrella policy becomes the underlying policy after the underlying liability policies have been exhausted, if the insured absorbs the first dollars of losses

Personal Umbrella Policy

An umbrella policy sits on top of your traditional business and/or personal liability insurance and only kicks in once those limits have been exceeded. For instance, suppose you have a policy that offers $1 million worth of legal liability protection. Now suppose your company gets sued and the plaintiff is awarded $2 million in damages. What would you do? If you only have the $1 million liability protection, you'll end up paying $1 million out of pocket. Now assume you have an umbrella policy up to $10 million as well. In this case, your standard policy would pay up to the first $1 million and the umbrella policy would cover the rest, up to its $10 million limit.

An umbrella policy is the cheapest means of acquiring additional substantial liability insurance for your home, vehicles, and business. Unfortunately, there is not a standard form of commercial liability insurance, so you will need to consult with your team of experts to determine the best policy for your business. Many of these policies will have substantial differences, however most policies provide coverage for personal injury liability, property damage liability, and advertising liability. Most of the time coverage is comprehensive, but is not "all-risk" since many contracts contain exclusions for liabilities from workers compensation, unemployment, and disability benefits law.[32]

Having your exit planner take a 30,000-foot view can make a big difference in the property/casualty area. Things look different from the mountaintop than they do driving through the forest. When you are so busy fighting in the trenches, you can lose sight of the battle plan. Too many wealthy families have no one who sees the whole picture. They have their business insurance specialist cover their commercial liability, they have their attorney review their legal documents, and they have their personal insurance agent sell them coverage, but no one reviews how all three work together. Over thirty years of working with business owners, I'm still astounded by the gaps in coverage I continually find with my clients. The risk they carry unaware is terrifying.

A BraveHeart Planning™ client from the South owned a large regional business. His business coverage was near spotless. There were one or two small issues, but overall the insurance agent had done a really nice job and seemed extremely competent. However, when I reviewed the personal coverage I found a whole different story. The next time my client came to my office, I asked him a suspiciously unassuming question: "Did you go to high school with your property/casualty insurance agent?"

He responded, "Yeah. How did you know that?"

I wanted to say, "Because your personal insurance coverage is a disaster." But I held my tongue and formulated a more diplomatic answer. "Because it looks like you have been sold the same type of coverage that you would have bought about the time you graduated high school. The problem is that when you bought this type of policy, you were worth thousands; but today, you are worth millions. I'm sure your insurance agent is a nice guy, but he is out of his league. You need a serious overhaul on your personal insurance."

"What do you mean?" he pondered confusedly. "I thought I had $10 million in liability coverage."

"Your business has $10 million in liability coverage. But your wife drives a car owned by you personally and it has very low liability limits. Let me ask you something: Do you know what would happen if your wife runs a red light and kills me?" (I know, it's a tough question, but these are the questions that must be addressed.)

He shook his head without saying anything.

"I'll tell you what will happen," I continued. "My wife will take a huge bite out of your family net worth and she might even become a very large shareholder in your company. Your personal insurance coverage won't be enough to cover my death in that situation and the business liability will not come into play to protect personal liability issues for you and your wife."

Think it can't happen to you? I had another client named Barry who owned a very large trucking company in Southern California. He came to me to do some business planning. I started by looking over his business insurances and found that his business liability coverage was woefully inadequate, in addition to the fact that he was not even incorporated. I asked Barry, "Why are you running a trucking company in California as a sole proprietorship? That makes absolutely no sense."

He told me that he had been advised by his CPA to remain a sole proprietorship because there was no tax reason to incorporate. He thought it was a waste of money.

I informed Barry that incorporation of a business is much more about providing limited liability to the business owner than it is saving taxes, especially in a litigious state like California. Besides, CPAs tend to make lousy lawyers and vice versa. I incorporated the business for Barry and I advised him to bump up his liability coverage. Providentially, Barry acted on my advice quickly.

Mere weeks later, one of Barry's trucks was involved in a horrible accident. Some steel bars broke free from the flatbed's trailer and fell onto the freeway. The bars bounced once on the road, up into the air, and through the windshield of the car driving behind. If I hadn't made sure Barry's insurance was where it needed to be, not only would he have likely been stripped of everything he owned, but also the injured family would not have been paid the money they needed to cover their losses, which were substantial. As it was, we settled the accident for the policy limits. The business survives today and the injured family was compensated to the extent money can compensate in a loss like that.

Life Insurance

There are two great constants in life: death and taxes. They happen to everyone, yet they are rarely talked about, especially death. People find death uncomfortable so they avoid the subject. Unfortunately, whether it is dealt with or not, premature death can have a very large financial impact on your family. We use life insurance to hedge against the financial impact of your death on your family and business.

People tend to think that if they are relatively young and healthy, they don't have to worry about death. The converse is actually true. The further away you are from retirement, the more need you have to protect against premature death. The reason is that even though your risk of dying is smaller when you are younger, it will have a much greater impact if it does. In insurance, they call this a high-risk, low-probability exposure.

Exposures that are unlikely to happen but carry severe repercussions should they occur, are precisely the kind of risks that are best taken care of with insurance. If a risk is a high probability but low impact, say a paper cut for a paper filer, it makes sense to simply bear the risk. If it is a high-impact, high-risk situation, it will probably be too expensive to insure, which is why acts of war are almost always excluded from insurance policies.

In its simplest form, life insurance is designed to replace the income that you would have earned if you had lived longer. I also use life insurance to cover a known cost that will not go away in the future, like estate taxes, or having cash in your estate to equalize inheritance for children.

Sitting down with your wealth manager to make sure your life insurance coverage is sufficient is very worthwhile. You may be surprised when you actually calculate your family's income needs. If you haven't thought about it in a while, you may need to reevaluate your coverage. After all, as your standard of living rises, so does your need for income replacement.

Vehicle Access and Insurance

Vehicles are one of the most widely owned and used major assets of consumers in the US.[33] For the average American, the car creates the greatest risk of economic loss in both property and liability damage. In some states, owners of vehicles may be liable for not only their own actions but also the negligent acts of family members, household members, and minors. In essence, both the owner of the vehicle and the driver are jointly liable for damages caused by the driver.

Managing risk in your vehicles encompasses more than just purchasing automobile insurance. You also need to maintain your vehicles in driving condition and educate your children about the dangers they will face on the roadways. Learning to drive is the first adult responsibility that most children face; as such, they often do not understand the severe consequences their decisions can have. Up until they turn sixteen, most children live in a protected bubble. They face consequences, but not many that are long-term. Young adults inherently do not understand that their mistakes on the road can follow them throughout the rest of their lives.

It was 5:30 p.m. when Aaron called me on my way to my anniversary dinner with my wife. He said, "The cops are holding Kurt out on a dirt road south of town. He's in trouble and I need your help now." I wheeled around and told my wife we would need to have our dinner date the following night.

Aaron's son, Kurt, had been driving his truck. Kurt turned onto a dirt road and a kid about sixteen years old driving a four-wheeler came from a side dirt road and turned in front of his truck. This kind of made Kurt mad and so he proceeded to run up on the kid and give him a little tap to the rear end of the four-wheeler with his bumper.

Things went downhill from there. The tap on the rear of the four-wheeler made the kid lose control and he ran off the road and was thrown off. Luckily, the four-wheeler did not hit him when he flew off. The kid's father drove up about that time in his truck and he was very mad. He called the cops and wanted to press charges for attempted murder or at least assault with a deadly weapon.

That is how the situation stood at the time I arrived. After understanding what had happened, I asked the father to take a little walk with me. We proceeded to walk and talk. I explained how Kurt's intent was not to harm the boy and that we could work out an apology and some community service or work around this man's farm if he would prefer. He had a chance to cool down and since his son only had mostly a scare, he agreed not to press charges. And just like that it was over. Kurt was lucky; the consequences of his actions could have easily involved jail time and definitely would have negatively affected his family.

I think it is important to communicate with our children very clearly the devastating consequences of reckless driving, texting while driving, speeding, and drunk driving, just to name a few. It is also best to not allow your children to let anyone else drive their vehicle, and I would caution them against driving someone else's. It may seem paranoid or heavy-handed, but my career as a lawyer and wealth manager has taught me that the risks are far too real. We have worked with hundreds of business owners to clean up their insurance and risk management, but there remain thousands out there who refuse to look into this vital area of business continuity planning. Too many of them have been hit by lawsuits that wiped them out, or they died without the proper controls in place to continue their business.

One such person was a guy I knew named Rob. Rob was a hard-working owner of a successful business. Like most entrepreneurs, he tended to make all the decisions himself. Because he was fifty-two, he thought he was far too young to be concerned with death. He did not know or plan for how that might impact his family or business. And then one day, he did not wake up.

Rob's death was a tragedy to his family, but he had made no plans for his business. Though his family was left with enough to survive via a retirement plan we had pushed him to fund and a decent life insurance policy, his failure to make any plans whatsoever for the business killed his company. No one knew what to do about whether they should try to continue or sell the business. He controlled everything, and so no one knew the overall financial condition of the business or anything else for that matter. The employees understood their jobs would not likely survive; they headed for the hills immediately, getting new jobs elsewhere. That was the end of the business. There was no chance for a sale or a continuation of the business to save employees' jobs or to realize any value from the business for the family. Rob had no plan to retain the employees or continue the company, so it folded. Contingency planning would have saved this business.

As a business owner, you are very familiar with contingency planning. It is likely that you prepare for a host of adverse scenarios so that your company will not be taken unaware by adverse business conditions. You need to apply that same level of planning and risk management to the risk of your own incapacitation or death.

CHAPTER 7

Living Your Legacy

70 A.D.–1948 A.D.

Empires have risen and fallen and been forgotten and destroyed, buried under the layers of civilizations that arose to take their place. One people group alone has kept their roots and their heritage. Many of them tracing their lineage further back than most governments have existed. Weaving in and out of world events, disappearing into the tapestry of world culture, yet still, the distinct thread of the Jewish people has remained for centuries.

In Exodus, we learn how the Jews escaped slavery from the Egyptians. The World Wars were marred by their deaths. Thrown into ghettos by nation after nation, hunted down, characterized as greedy, miserly and controllers of the world's finances, many have sworn to stamp them out. Hitler himself boldly declared, "The result of this war will be the complete annihilation of the Jews." But none have succeeded in their quest. Time and time again, when hope seemed all but lost, the Jewish people have survived.

No other people group has lasted as have they. For millennia, their culture, religion, and even their resourcefulness have stood the test of time. Despite intense persecution, a lack of country to call their own, and downright annihilation tactics by some of the world's governments, they remain. Currently residing in 135 countries, 97 have permanent organizations in order to maintain their community, retaining a bond that is unlike any other. The network of Jews worldwide is astounding, their connections to one another strong, and their legacy enduring."

The Jewish people are a group that embodies the term "legacy." They have held onto their history, heritage, and family identity through thousands of years of persecution and dispersion. Think about that. One of the most influential groups of all time started as one family of sheepherders in the middle of the desert. Talk about leaving a legacy! Just imagine having the kind of world impact those patriarchs had. Their descendants wound up controlling substantial philanthropic efforts and major industries, including medicine, banking and finance, throughout the world, because they embraced stewardship. While legacy is the concept at the heart of the BraveHeart Planning Process™, it is inextricably linked with the idea of stewardship.

Stewardship is a word that is somewhat outdated in the modern world; certainly the term is seldom used. In America, it is a word reminiscent of the days of aristocracy, slaves, and injustice. We rightly shrink from such negative connotations, but stewardship is a concept that predates the American Revolution and even Europe itself. No matter what word you use—accountability, responsibility, or stewardship—taking care of your money for your family is as important today as it ever was. In a world of rampant overspending by the consumer, fiscal irresponsibility by the government, and reckless risk-taking by the private sector, the careful steward is a dying breed.

> **No matter what word you use – accountability, responsibility, or stewardship – taking care of your family's wealth is as important today as ever.**

Stewardship is not lost though. Most high net-worth individuals are highly competent caretakers of resources; however, stewardship applies to more than just those with vast resources. Whether you are single or married, rich or poor, young or old, you have resources that have been entrusted to you, monetarily and otherwise.

Making your money count involves taking responsibility where you are right now with the assets that you have been entrusted with today. Though responsible investing is a big part of it, wise stewardship is about more than just taking care of your money—it involves many facets of life, such as your talents and time. You can give in so many more ways than materially. You are more than your net worth. Most people understand time to be the most valuable commodity. Donate your time and talents to the next generation: coach a children's basketball team, mentor a younger business associate or volunteer for the community. Your abilities and money are gifts that have been given to you for a purpose.

Don't forget to give. On top of benefiting others' lives, donating brings deeper satisfaction and enjoyment. Relinquishing a portion of your income can teach you and your family valuable lessons in stewardship. Those who make money their sole aim are never good stewards and often fail to leave positive legacies. But if you can give your dollars away freely, you are telling money that it has no power over you!

A family that neglects to steward the hearts and minds of its members fails to build interfamilial relationships. That family will ultimately crumble. Any family failure is heartbreaking, but when a family has built up significant resources, the breakdown becomes a public catastrophe. *The Wall Street Journal* and other publications are full of stories detailing the bitter feuding between families of fortune.

Every family fights, but not every family has the resources to take that fight to the next level. Throw substantial money into the mix, and all of a sudden your heirs have the resources to hire lawyers, go to court, and destroy businesses and charitable organizations.

If you wait until you are near death to communicate the principles of stewardship to your family members, it is already too late. Building a legacy of wise decisions and counsel for your family is not something that you can save until later. Some personal friends of mine are still struggling to forgive their parents for tearing apart their family by fighting over inheritance in court. Don't let that be you!

Legacy is not something you can save for later.

Family is at the heart of the BraveHeart Process because if you get the family part wrong, it doesn't matter how well the rest of the process goes. You will not be remembered for the size of your balance sheet, but rather for the impact you made on people and the legacy you left through your children. Everyone, regardless of the size of his bank account, has a chance to leave a legacy. The only thing holding you back is the amount of work you are willing to put in. Your success creating a family legacy is directly proportional to how well you plan, prepare, and execute the legacy building process.

"Legacy building" is the shepherding of a family that creates heirs who regularly contribute to the financial, human, intellectual, spiritual and social capital of their families and community. They are connected to their extended families and work hard to grow their family relations and encourage generational growth. They are taught to be thankful to God above for the blessings he has bestowed upon them and they embrace their responsibility to love their neighbors, understanding that it is more blessed to give than it is to receive. They work to develop the competencies to handle the responsibilities of wealth and effectively utilize the opportunities that are available.

A business owner who builds a successful legacy doesn't have family that simply relies on him and his wealth, but rather build things of their own, whether that is careers, businesses, arts, or charities. Families of legacy refuse to be owned by their wealth. Instead, they put it to work to make a difference in their families, their communities, and the world at large.

> **Families with legacy refuse to be owned by their wealth.**

The Legacy Family

It is my experience that families spend much more time trying to build a successful business than a successful family...but Legacy Families are unafraid to serve, brave enough to forgive, and bold enough to build. A Legacy Family is a family that embodies the principles of the BraveHeart Process. Though the process is original to me, the principles are timeless.

Legacy Families aren't created overnight, and they certainly do not happen by accident. The foundation of the family is the strength of the marriage between mom and dad. If that marriage is a loving, supportive, and forgiving relationship, where they invest time in each other's lives, then it is very likely that they will, in turn create children much like themselves.

Henry Jones is the head one of my favorite Legacy Families. When he was in his late 40s, Henry and his wife lost everything they had due to a joint venture that went bad. Rather than give up, the Joneses stayed together and worked to rebuild. Henry was able to rebuild so successfully that he ended up with more than he started. Today, he enjoys a thriving legacy that will continue for generations. The road was hard, but Henry and his wife persevered when lesser men and women would have quit.

Henry and his wife have exhibited such a love for each other that many envy their happiness. But few know the hard road they have traveled. They taught their children well. They imprinted the ideas of family legacy on their children and the children grew up working alongside their parents, learning the family business, and raising a family. And though they are financially successful, it is clear that the real wealth of the family is founded on genuine affection for each other and an abiding faith in God.

Their children are continuing the family legacy by exposing the grandchildren to the same kind of experiences and teaching. They are investing their time, talents, and finances into the next generation, without forgetting the most important part to them: faith in God and in his Son, Jesus Christ.

So now that you've seen an example, just how does one build a family that remains profitable, successful, healthy, loving and content, for not just one, but many generations? How does one ensure that the family does not just have money, but also capacity, connection, compassion, and competency? The key to having a family like this is to raise the children in a positive environment where unconditional love is granted, faith in God is modeled, and forgiveness is practiced. There is an expectation of each one doing their best at whatever they undertake. They are taught to respect those in authority over them and to obey their parents. These disciplines are blended together with the creation of a combination of hard and soft structures as needed.

Before I dive into a few of these structures, I do want to give a word of warning. No matter how well you plan and execute, there is no guarantee of success because the actions of your family members are outside of your control. Every person will make his own choice. You can guide, lead, and be an example to your children, but your children can reject your values and your faith despite your best efforts. Your job is to raise your children in the best way you know how, to teach them, to show them the truth, and to do your best. But how it all turns out is beyond your control. Results belong to God alone; your job is to give it your best and lead by example.

I counseled a dentist a year or so ago. He is an honorable man, who is well respected and a hard worker. He and his wife raised three beautiful children. But during college, one of the daughters became trapped in drug addiction. It has become a living nightmare for the man and his wife. The problem continues to this day. The daughter is about fifty now and she is still caught in the world of drug addiction. Her lifestyle choice has caused continued conflict between her father and mother, as one wants to cut off the daughter and the other wants to make sure she is cared for. There is a granddaughter that is involved, which further complicates the matter.

Not all problems will go away simply because you plan and execute well. That being said, having the following structures in place will go a long way toward building a family legacy that lasts:

- Family Meeting

- Investment Committee

- Strategic Plan

- Family Constitution

- Family Governance

Family Meeting

The very first step to building a family legacy is the family meeting. Family meetings are designed to deal with the "business of the family." It is a structured discussion time that typically involves all members of the family, and should be done on a regular basis. Hopefully you are able to institute these meetings while your children are young so that there is a format and structure in place that they will be comfortable with when they become adults. Family meetings can cover a wide range of topics including weekend plans, responsibility delegation, vacation planning, philanthropy and other projects. Naturally as the family gets larger and takes on more responsibility, these meetings will get more formal and the topics more serious.

We have held family meetings with our children since they could carry on a conversation. We use this time to catch up on what everyone is doing, what plans are for the coming weeks or months, and what issues they are being faced with at work, school, or church. If there is conflict in the family, we seek to resolve it.

Sometimes we are negotiating a new schedule for chores. Other times we are discussing what we want to give to charity and which ones we want to include. We celebrate academic and athletic success and the things we see positive in what they do and the choices they make.

We will sometimes include others that may be visiting with us in our family meetings, though we tend to keep those meetings on the lighter side. We are aware that our guests have generally never seen anything like it.

The older the children get, the more we include financial discussions. We explain the challenges of making, managing, and investing money. When we are facing difficult times or challenges, we have not hidden those from the children. They are made aware, to the extent they are old enough to deal with it. We pray about those challenges together.

We almost always read the Bible together, discuss it, and then we pray for each other. We like to sing together too. Everyone participates, no matter how old or how young. In our family meeting, we are training the next generation to live and grow our family legacy. We like frequent family meetings, with business issues being included only as needed. We do not want the family meetings to be taken over by business. In our meetings, it is God first, family second, and business third.

The key steps to an effective family meeting are:

- Establish a specific regular meeting time and place, and keep this appointment as you would any other important scheduled activity

- Develop ground rules

- Give the floor to members one at a time so that everyone gets a chance to voice an opinion or share their thoughts

- Do not interrupt when someone else is talking

- Avoid being either too domineering or too diffident

- Avoid putdowns, dismissals, patronization, or sarcasm

- Always begin each meeting with everyone giving something positive that has occurred in their lives for which they are thankful

- Make sure you celebrate the successes of the family members no matter how young

In addition, as the children become adults, you should develop written agendas, rotate leadership of the meeting, keep notes in a record book, document decisions, and plan a fun activity afterwards if time permits, like a family game night or movie night. It is important that with any problem or issue that is discussed in the meeting, you utilize a concrete decision-making process to overcome challenges. The process should work through these five problem-solving steps:

1. What do we have?

2. What do we want?

3. How can we get there?

4. By when?

5. How will we evaluate our success?[34]

Regardless of how many issues you solve at a meeting, it will still be a failure if you do not properly communicate. Caring communication and concern for each other is at the heart of successful family legacy building.

At no time is this more important than at family meetings. Family meetings can often serve as flash points for interfamily conflict, lighting fires that can easily result in "the family meltdown." One moment you're happily recounting family memories, and the next minute Sandy is screaming at her brother Jim for marrying Jane who's ruining her relationship with

Mom. Family relationships are complicated, to say the least, but the more you focus on loving one another, the smaller the other problems become.

For families that work together, the potential to blow up is even worse. After an entire year of stuffing aggravating issues down in the interest of business, family meetings can seem like the perfect time to air long-standing grievances. A conflict can start with something small and then escalate quickly.

Family meltdowns can surface out of nowhere, sometimes in the exact moment when everyone seems to be getting along well. Although the conflict is triggered by a small slight, it's rarely the true problem. In fact, the issue that begins the fight is often just a proxy battle for larger issues within the family that run deep. The issues can range from favoritism and competition to an imbalance of power in the family network.

If you want to preserve the peace at the family meeting, and look back with fondness on your time, then you need to be prepared. If a conflict does surface, remain calm. Someone is going to have to act with self-control to put the sparks out, so it might as well be you.

Above all, remain humble. Nothing destroys family legacies like pride. It's a corrosive agent that can tear apart a lifetime of work and energy. Conflict is no fun, but it can be constructive if the family takes the time to listen and deal with the issues calmly and rationally.

Investment Committee

Investment committees come in a variety of flavors. They can be as sophisticated as the professional management team of a single-family office for a billionaire or they can be as simple as an informal single-family unit committee made up of the parents and the children. For the $5-$50 million range, investment committees tend to have a mix of family and nonfamily professional members. Nonfamily members of the investment committee may include your wealth manager, CPA, or other trusted professionals. The basic intent of an investment committee is to advise the wealth creator on investment decision-making.

You may not think that your family has enough wealth to warrant an investment committee, or you may reason (and rightly so) that you are quite competent enough to manage your own investments. Whether that is the case or not, an investment committee is beneficial for families because it is a great way to train children into a Legacy Family mindset. By allowing your children to sit on the investment committee once they reach a certain age (usually decided by the parents in an informal family or the family constitution in a structured family), you will be able to teach them your work ethic, investment philosophy, and decision-making criteria while they are still young.

Another good reason to institute a family investment committee is that it provides a fertile training ground for your family members so that they will be able to function effectively when you are not around. If you introduce your children to the family investment committee while they are still young, by the time you retire from family affairs, they will have had decades of experience making investment decisions. When a first generation wealth creator dies or steps back from leading the family it creates a vacuum that must be filled. It will make your transition a hundred times smoother if you create an investment council to fill that void years in advance of it happening.

Strategic Plan

The next step to building a family legacy is to create a strategic plan. As a business owner, you are no doubt familiar with strategic plans. But have you considered writing one specifically for your family? In order for your family to succeed, you will need to create a communication process, establish benchmarks to evaluate progress, and monitor and reevaluate the plan on an ongoing basis.

Now of course, a family is not the same as a business. You can't fire your children if they don't fall into line, and you can't use your position to get what you want from your spouse. Families are going to have different challenges and emotional issues than a business, but that doesn't mean they don't need to plan. In fact, I would argue that a family is much more difficult to run than a business and therefore requires more planning, not less!

A strategic plan is not a short-term plan, but rather it is intended to span the generations. If handled well, your legacy can impact your progeny for many generations. The strategic plan is based on family values, not on wealth. It should encompass the family vision, which serves as the driver of everything the family does; the mission statement, which gives the family a focus for what needs to be done to accomplish the family mission; the statement of values, which gives the family a common ground to rally around; the definition of family, which gives parameters for whom is included in the family and why; the allocation of capital, which establishes priorities for the utilization of resources; and finally governance and leadership, which outlines family succession, decision-making, and arbitration of conflict.

It does take some investigation and frank discussion about what your family needs and what they are willing to adopt in order to strengthen the family generationally. Whatever the strategic plan is, the family needs to buy-in to the plan for it to be effective.

The people most likely to implement the structures and longer term planning for the family are what we call "Family Stewards." Family Steward is a term adopted by Russ Alan Prince, a leading researcher in the world of high-net worth and ultra-high net worth individuals and families. Prince has surveyed hundreds of millionaires and billionaires. Based on his extensive research, Prince categorizes investors and business owners into nine high net-worth personalities.[xxxv]

The characteristics of the Family Steward according to Russ Alan Prince are as follows:

- Dominant focus is to take care of their families

- Conservative in personal and professional life

- Generally still married to their first spouse

Family Constitution

If the strategic plan is like a roadmap, then the constitution is like the train tracks that keep the locomotive on course and heading in the right direction. Every country has a constitution, every organized club has bylaws, but most families just have the parents making it up as they go along. It's not necessarily a bad thing to have mom and dad make the rules as they come up, but it's much better to have a written, agreed-upon constitution. It is in the written form that the organization of a successful family is passed down. That does not mean there is no flexibility, for flexibility can be important. The constitution can be amended as time reveals issues you or your forbears did not anticipate—but it also protects the family from sudden decisions without the benefit of the family history and wisdom.

The family constitution sets down the rules for which family governance, power sharing, communication, and problem-solving systems are established in a concrete and definitive way. Now, if you are a first generation business owner, this may seem a little intense, especially if your children are still young. In your case, a strategic plan may merely outline your values and mission.

The need for increased complexity of planning rises with increasing family wealth. Though we like to keep things simple, simple is only good where it is adequate to handle your family's needs.

In truth, a family constitution is not for everyone. The importance of this tool grows as the size and the wealth of the family multiplies. Determining what you need and when you need it is best considered with your qualified professional team.

Family Governance

The final vital soft structure that needs to be implemented to create a lasting family legacy is the family governance structure. Family governance is easy in the first generation. The owner is usually the one who leads the family. He makes the decisions and everyone else falls into line. Once the owner is gone, however, there can be a power struggle if the proper protocols are not already put into place.

Like any business, families need strong, capable, and assertive leaders. Leaders set agendas, call meetings, hold people accountable, and enforce the rules. Leadership is a tad more complicated in a family than a business. No one can be fired from the family. There are ways to keep people in line, but it is certainly much harder to do when you have less leverage over your family members, particularly if you are not the founding or first generation of the family.

The larger the family, the more need there is for leadership. With each passing generation, the family grows and simple governance structures fall by the wayside. If a formal system is not put into place, chaos will follow. There are many different strategies for family leadership, but some of the most popular are the family executive, the family council, and the family office.

Under the Family Executive plan, family members elect a leader who is responsible to the family and replaceable by the adult members. In essence, the family acts as the board of directors and elects a CEO of the family. The advantage of this structure is that, since it relies on the decision-making of a single person, decisions are made quickly and decisively. The disadvantage to this style is that relying on one person restricts access to leadership and can result in a loss of voice for many family members.

Larger and wealthier families (usually families of three generations or more) often adopt the Family Council plan. Under Family Council governance, each wing of the family picks one representative to sit on the family council to vote on issues. The final decision is determined by majority rule. The Family Council strategy allows decisions to be made democratically. No single family member can run amok. The scope of one person's authority and the extent that he can exercise discretion in business or family matters is subject to the oversight of the family council. They are the ones who approve strategy and budget and make important financial decisions. The disadvantage to the family council is that decision-making is slow and bureaucratic. There is a greater chance for family politics to get carried away and for conflict to happen.

The third strategy for family governance is to create a family office. In order for the implementation of family decisions to run smoothly, wealthy families often outsource the tactical financial decisions to a family office. A family office is a group of dedicated professionals who oversee the "empire" as it were and ensure that everything runs the way it is supposed to. Family offices will coordinate and/or provide accounting, legal, investment management, and administrative services for the family.

They come in two primary flavors: the single-family office and the multi-family office. In a single-family office, the entire staff serves a single family, whereas a multi-family office takes care of a number of families. The extent of services provided depends on the particular family office. Some of them even provide a communal jet or yacht that can be used by member families. The advantage of the family office is that it provides technical and financial expertise that members of the family typically do not have.

It is never too late to make the ones you love a priority. Build a family of wealth instead of just a wealthy family. This is a mission worth pursuing. The rewards are rich and loving relationships and productive citizens for generations. Those who choose to accept this mission will find it requires intentional planning, lots of hard work, and a willingness to give of your time, your energy and your love.

> **Those who choose to accept this mission will find it requires intentional planning, lots of hard work, and a willingness to risk it all in order to win it all.**

One such family of wealth I respect is the Hall family.

In 1910, J.C. Hall founded Hallmark at the age of eighteen. He stepped off a train from Nebraska in Kansas City, Missouri, with not much more than two shoeboxes of picture postcards. From that humble beginning, the company has grown into multi-billion dollar businesses. The empire includes both Hallmark Cards, Inc. and the Hallmark Hall of Fame television series.

The cards are always high in quality and honorable in every way. The television productions are based on three principles: quality, good taste, and enriching relationships.

What J.C. Hall created, succeeding generations have nurtured. There has always been a Hall in top leadership. Today, the Chairman of the board is Donald J. Hall. His sons hold the following positions: Donald J. Hall, Jr. is president and CEO and David E. Hall is president of the company's North America division.

The family and the company are bound together by Hallmark's stated beliefs and values.

Beliefs

- That our products and services must enrich people's lives

- That creativity and quality—in our products, services and all that we do—are essential to our success

- That innovation in all areas of our business is essential to attaining and sustaining leadership

- That the people of Hallmark are our company's most valuable resource

- That distinguished financial performance is imperative to accomplish our broader purpose

- That our private ownership must be preserved

Values

- Excellence in all we do

- High standards of ethics and integrity

- Caring and responsible corporate citizenship for Kansas City and for each community in which we operate

- These beliefs and values guide our business strategies, our corporate behavior, and our relationships with business partners, suppliers, customers, communities and each other

We celebrate those that have gone on before us and successfully blazed the trail. We can learn valuable lessons by studying their successes. You can live a legacy and you can leave one. For it to be successful, your legacy cannot be driven by the money. If that is all you leave, it will destroy the family eventually. How many truly wealthy families are great families that love each other and celebrate their successes? As you read this book, don't just consider the large business issues, but also consider the family legacy issues.

CHAPTER 8

Transition to Family

London, England, 1170 A.D.

Romanticized by his people and minstrels alike, Richard the Lionheart was larger than life. Standing over 6'5", with red gold hair, blue eyes, and bulging muscles, he certainly looked the part. Richard had a reputation for military prowess and fearlessness that bordered on foolishness. He had the keen mind of a skilled commander, and the disciplined body of a champion fighter. His foremost foe, Saladin of Egypt, respected him greatly, and even sent him two replacements when he lost his horse in battle. He put down rebellion in Gascony, conquered the island of Sicily, captured the town of Acre, and almost retook Jerusalem, but he is perhaps best known for his role in the Robin Hood legend. Richard was loved by his people and respected by his enemies.

But his family hated him.

He was born the third son of King Henry II, and was never expected to ascend the throne of England. Richard grew up in England but he spent most of his life in France, living in Aquitaine, the homeland of his mother. Richard was the favorite son of his mother, Eleanor, which sparked most of the conflict with his father and brothers.

In 1170, King Henry II decided to divide his kingdom between his three eldest surviving sons: Henry the Young King, Richard, and Geoffrey. Henry crowned his oldest son, Henry the Young, as King of England, but he bequeathed his territories in France to his two other sons. King Henry II still retained ultimate control over his possessions, though, including the all-important purse strings.

Henry's motivation for splitting up his kingdom while he was alive remains a mystery, lost in the annals of history. He may have wanted to slow down as he got older or perhaps give his sons limited leadership experience under his protection. No matter the intent, the changing of the guard certainly did not go according to Henry's plan. His sons became disenchanted with the status quo almost immediately after the division. They chafed under their father's heavy-handed control. Not content to wait for their father's death, all three sons rose up in rebellion to take the kingdom from King Henry II while he was still alive.

Henry II responded with speed, brutality, and overwhelming force. He quickly crushed the rebellion, forcing his sons to beg for forgiveness and sue for peace. Henry spared their lives, but took away most of their land. In a peculiar move of cruelty, Henry forced Richard to punish the barons that had joined him in rebellion against his father. In order to ensure Richard's compliance, Henry kept Richard's mother Eleanor hostage for the rest of her life. Richard eventually found some semblance of peace with his father, but the infighting and political intrigue would continue amongst the family for the rest of their lives. Even the brothers who fought alongside each other soon turned against each other.

It wasn't until all three of Richard's familial rivals died that he had peace in his family. With the death of Henry II, Geoffrey, and Henry the Young, Richard was left King of England, a title he never expected to hold. Court life didn't suit Richard the Lionheart well, however, and it wasn't long before the warrior-king thirsted for battle. A short while after ascending the throne, Richard donned the Crusader cross and left Prince John as steward of England.

The Lionheart experienced great military success in his campaign against the Saladin, but it wasn't long before he offended his French and Austrian allies, causing them to sail home. Left alone in the Holy Land with only a small force of loyal followers, Richard was forced to abandon the conquest of Jerusalem. He eventually made his way back to the European continent, but on his journey home he was ambushed by Austrians and handed over to the Holy Roman Emperor and imprisoned. In Richard's absence, Prince John seized the throne, oppressed the people of England, and left Richard to rot in prison. The only truly loving relationship Richard seems to have had was with his mother, who raised an obscenely expensive ransom to release him. A Prominent British Historian named Steven Runciman delivered this final

*verdict of Richard I: "He was a bad son, a bad husband, and a bad king,
but a gallant and splendid soldier."*[35i]

Richard was a Lionheart, but he was no BraveHeart. He loved to battle,
but only for the thrill of victory. In family business, it isn't enough to
fight; you have to fight for something. Richard won almost every battle he
engaged in, but he lost in the things that mattered most. Though Richard
was the ideal warrior, he was a poor sovereign and an even worse family
man. He infuriated his allies, impoverished his kingdom, jeopardized the
lives of his men, and destroyed his family relations. If you make a lot of
money, become the man in charge and exit while still on top, but lose
the succession battle, it will all be for naught.

Succession has caused more wars and pain than perhaps any other single
event. Henry II's poor planning and heavy-handed leadership style
sparked a rebellion and almost cost him a kingdom. Planning ahead,
managing leadership transition, and knowing who is in charge at the
changing of the guard will go a long way toward maintaining order and
profitability in your business.

I have been a part of countless transitions in my career. Sometimes, the
family transitions are the most difficult to pull off successfully. Why is
that the case? You'd think that transitioning to like-minded individuals
who love you and work together with you would be a walk in the park,
but that isn't exactly the case. The problem is that you also have to wade
through family conflict, emotions, sentiments, and all the mess that comes
with being a family on top of all the financial, legal, tax, and cash flow
issues that you will have to deal with in any business transition.

Transitioning your business to your children or other family members
is not simply a matter of finances or tax savings. Your family may
maintain professionalism in their work, civility in their relationships,
and understanding in their communication with each other, but when
the time for your exit arrives, it can be a whole new ball game. Not only
does your exit bring up a great number of new issues to fight over, but
it can also reveal underlying conflicts.

During a transition process, family conflicts can threaten to derail the
entire process. The key to smoothing relationships and maintaining
transition momentum is the understanding that the problem at hand

is rarely the true issue. Business families have the tendency to suppress problems in the name of professionalism and keeping the peace. The problem is that a change as large as a transition is bound to open up old wounds. Sometimes any change in relationship can cause old struggles to resurface. Your exit has the potential to turn into a power struggle no matter how much your family members love each other.

> **The key to smoothing relationships and maintaining transition momentum is the understanding that the problem at hand is rarely the true issue.**

Family Leadership Transitions

Even within the choice to leave your business to family, there may be a lot of flexibility. You don't have to dump the business on your children and then hop the next plane to the Bahamas. As with every step in the BraveHeart Planning Process™, you are in charge here. You have complete control over where, how, and when you exit. Some ways are better than others, and I would advise against some of these transition strategies, but in the end it is up to you how you structure your exit.

Though each situation is unique, The Family Business Institute[36i] lists five common ways that family business owners exit, with some colorful names to describe them:

1. Cold Turkey

2. Delay, Delay, and...

3. Here, Gone, Here, Gone...

4. Non-family CEO

5. Gradual/Progressive

With the "cold turkey" method, the CEO maintains control until he dies, falls ill, has an accident, or some other unfortunate set of events forces him to relinquish control suddenly. The successor is then forced to assume complete and total control immediately, with little preparation. I like to call this tactic "Baptism by Fire." We wouldn't generally advise implementing the Baptism by Fire method, but it does have one advantage: the family does not have to endure the conflicts that so often accompany a phase transition while the leader is letting go and the successor is acquiring more responsibility.

The downside to the Baptism by Fire method is obviously that the successor is suddenly thrust into a leadership position for which he is ill-equipped. Some successors will bear the burden and somehow manage to survive against the odds, but many will fail, as they have no chance to acquire the experience they so desperately need before they take the reins and full weight of responsibility. I know of some businesses where the children actually retired before the parents did! When that happens, the business is left with no leadership and no succession plans. If your desire is to leave your business to your children, you must develop the leadership skills within your children or grandchildren. This will not happen by accident.

Naturally many leaders are wary of going cold turkey so they swing to the other extreme and delay, delay, delay. I call it the "Mañana Motion" (as in "I'll leave *mañana*," which is Spanish for "tomorrow"). Under this tactic, owners retain complete control but keep promising to transition. At various points, some control is transferred to the successor, but complete control is never quite granted. The delay game really doesn't have any advantages. Instead, it frustrates any potential successors, making them bitter, not to mention a flight risk. Delaying does not inspire the kind of legacy we are talking about creating for the family.

Whenever a mañana leader finally passes away or hands the reins over, the successor may be so conditioned to follow that he doesn't want to lead. Leadership needs to be developed by slowly giving increasingly more responsibility to the successor along the way, with teaching at each succeeding level. I have had many clients who managed the gradual transition wonderfully, but one of the best was a man named Mark.

Mark is a client of ours that owns a large plumbing contractor business. His son, Julian, has been groomed for twenty-five years to take this business over. Julian started working in the field as a support person for the plumbers when he was in high school. Upon his graduation from college, he decided to come back and make plumbing his life's work.

After ten years of training and helping the business grow, Julian was given a substantial ownership stake in the business. Mark retired a few years ago and Julian, who now owns 40 percent, runs the business, and has doubled its size within the last five years.

Mark has put plans in place to transition the rest of the business to Julian at Mark's death. Julian's siblings, who chose not to work in the business, have been provided for in other ways. This is a good example of someone who made a plan, developed the management skills in his son, and who has preserved the family relationships by dealing with the process in an open manner with the rest of the family.

Another tactic that some owners are fond of is the aptly named "Here, Gone, Here, Gone" method. If I were to name this one I'd call it "The Cat Came Back" because in this tactic, the leader turns over control very quickly, hops on a plane or boat for an extended vacation, and then returns suddenly to reassert control. He may periodically retreat to a seasonal residence or take a sabbatical, but at the end of his trip, he always shows back up at the business. When the past leader returns, he usually changes initiatives and projects that have been implemented in his absence. Some owners never even bother to change titles when they return, preferring to be the absentee master commander.

The Cat Came Back is probably the most destructive of the transition strategies. While the successor does gain some experience—and succession does in fact occur, at least for a while—the Here Gone Gambit may cause the successor to get fed up and leave. Key employees are also tempted to leave, as they are pulled in two directions. No one likes to be placed in the middle of a conflict. What is even more discouraging for the employees is to see the initiatives they've worked so hard on under the successor, undermined or removed by the reappearing leader who can't seem to let go.

The fourth option is to place into position a Non-family CEO. I call this the "Transition CEO." In this case, you transfer control to someone outside the family (who assumes effective control around the second year), while you gradually withdraw and complete your transition by year four. Once you are gone, the non-family CEO begins to mentor your successor, who assumes control when the non-family CEO retires at year three to seven. This option is a clear win for families who have successors that are clearly interested in running the business, but not quite ready to be handed the reins. It also allows the interim CEO to help train the successor to develop the skills needed to be the next family leader. A bonus is that a respected non-family leader can introduce new skills to the business and implement needed innovations and changes much more easily than a fresh, and rather green, successor.

The final transition strategy is the Gradual/Progressive approach, or what I would call the "Wise Approach." As is obvious from my moniker, this method is my favorite. With the Wise Approach, you gradually cede more and more responsibility to your successor. Somewhere between year five and ten, you will be completely unnecessary to the future staying power of the business, at which point you step aside completely.

If you still want to be involved, however, you are welcome to stay on in a consulting or advising position. If you do it correctly, no one will even notice the change because it will happen so smoothly. The advantage to this tactic is that the successor gains experience gradually, using the time to absorb the lessons of leadership. Plus, with fewer responsibilities, you are able to explore the options for your next stage of life on a limited basis.

The downside to the gradual approach is that there is plenty of opportunity for conflict and tension. As authority is handed off, one responsibility at a time, there is potential for friction and impatience on both sides. You may also feel like you are getting pushed aside, and it can be very easy to feel protective over the company that you built from the ground up.

Despite the downsides, I believe that the gradual transition is the right choice for most family businesses. Leaving "cold turkey" is asking for failure. The non-family CEO approach works well, but requires just the right person. The Delay Method and Here Again Gone Again approaches both can be disastrous. In my experience, allowing the successor to grow into his role is a great way for him to truly learn how to be an effective executive. That being said, you cannot simply designate a successor and expect him to learn everything on his own. Too many family businesses give the successor a broad title like executive vice president and then let him drift through his career without assuming authority over anything.

A better way is giving the successor new responsibilities one by one, a process I like to call grooming.

Grooming

As I have stated before, you have less than a 40 percent chance of successfully transferring your business to the next generation. In fact, you have a better chance of getting cancer than having your business outlast you! How can that be? At first, 40 percent seems like such a small percentage. But when one considers the dangers in the succession process, it is a wonder that even 40 percent actually do make it!

Consider the potential threats to a successful transition: rival potential successors, an unprepared, under-respected, or unenthusiastic successor, or no suitable successor at all. In the worst-case scenario, the owner dies suddenly without designating a successor and leaves a power vacuum, which is a potential litigation nightmare.

Publically-traded companies understand the pitfalls to successor transitions and take great pains to be ready. They run senior management candidates through an extensive and often exhausting selection process, vetting their credentials, speaking to their former employers, and giving them trial tasks to see if they are ready.

> **When a family business executive fails, the family itself is threatened.**

The process to select a leader for a family business needs to be just as thorough, for the stakes are just as high. When a public company executive fails, people lose their jobs and investors lose their money. When a family business executive fails, the family itself is threatened. With so much at stake, it is more important than ever to institute a successor-grooming program with the following steps.

Start with Employment

The leader of a family business must know the business inside and out in order to gain buy-in from key stakeholders. In a blue-collar business, that means working his way from the ground up, learning what it takes to accomplish each and every job in the company. In a white-collar business, it often involves obtaining the right credentials, experience, and producing key results.

It is never too early to start grooming your successor. If you plan on leaving the business to your children, then have them work in your business when they are young. Give them increasing responsibility and higher roles as they grow. Also assign them a mentor at each department where they work, so that by the time they take over the company, they know it better than you do.

Maintain Accountability

If you are going to have family members work in your business, you need to lay out some ground rules. What are the qualifications for eligibility? Can any family member get a job at the company, or will there be certain stipulations they have to meet first? Many families put a clause in their family constitution that outlines the job application procedure so that it is fair and equitable for family members and employees.

Once your potential successor gets a job in your company, you must also have a system in place to keep him accountable. Mixing business and family is bound to result in a tangle of emotions. Performance evaluations can easily feel like personal attacks, and substandard results often ensue. To keep this from happening, many family businesses require family employees to report to a nonfamily manager.

The bottom line is that when dealing with employees, whether family or not, you must keep it businesslike. If you don't treat your children like other employees, nonfamily employees will start resenting them. Additionally, giving family special treatment only harms their self-worth. Nothing is a better confidence booster to a child than knowing that he got the job because he earned it.

Compensate Accordingly

Once the right accountability is in place, appropriate and commensurate compensation is vital. Family businesses tend to fall off the wagon on one of two sides. They either over-compensate family members merely because of their status as relatives, or they undercompensate family members with the rationale that the business will eventually belong to them anyway.

Both ideas are dangerous. If you overcompensate, nonfamily members will become resentful and may even leave. If you undercompensate, family members will become resentful and leave. Obviously, it is up to you to decide, but the pay grade should be fair whether an employee is a part of the family or not.

Award Appropriately

Speaking of compensation, if pay should be fair, then so should ownership. Long before your transition, you need to decide if ownership should be gifted to family employees or if they will need to buy in. The ownership issue is unique to each family situation. Some families give ownership to nonbusiness family, while others gift the business to family employees and leave passive assets to the other family members. The problem is that business valuation is a moving target, so it can be very difficult to give equal gifts in different types of assets. Sometimes the business far outgrows investment funds, whereas other times the business is a time-consuming, labor-intensive machine that causes more worries than it is worth.

If you are struggling to pick a successor, a standardized grooming procedure can actually make the decision much easier. By starting early and training potential successors as you go, you will be able to simultaneously weed out any disinterested heirs and equip the committed ones. Over time, it will probably become clear who is best suited to run the company based on previous track record. If one clear heir apparent doesn't emerge, treat it is a blessing in disguise. Now instead of one committed family member to rely on, your business will rest on the shoulders of a committed core.

Grooming a successor is a vital part of the BraveHeart Planning Process™, and much like the rest of the process, the sooner you start, the better. Remember, retirement doesn't always happen when you expect it. With rising life expectancy, plummeting retirement benefits, and a tepid economic environment, it is no longer a simple matter of retiring at sixty-five and then living out your golden years on a golf course in Florida. In fact, retirement gets exponentially more complex and nuanced within the framework of business ownership. Just when is the right time to hand over the reins? It's not an easy decision, but with the right planning in place, it doesn't have to be agonizing. To help you plan your exit, check out these three timeless principles.

Don't Wait

Begin the process of transitioning your business long before you actually do. The best exit plans are begun seven to ten years before the actual sale or succession. Figuring you will get to it eventually, or that the transition will work itself out, is a recipe for failure. Choosing not to choose is still a choice, albeit a bad one. The best way to make your exit smooth is to institute a managed succession process, whereby control is handed over gradually as you move slowly to an advisory or rainmaker role.

Before you can institute that process, however, you will need to create a management-training program for your successor. As we've mentioned before, your successor needs to understand the business from the bottom up. In fact, it is vitally important that his training covers the breadth of the business, including all of the departments. If your successor has worked his way up in one department and is already a manager, it may be necessary to send him back down to receive bottom level training in other departments.

You will also need to assign mentors or managers to train him at each level. It should be no surprise to your employees that a family-member is being groomed to take over. To make the transition smoother, they will have much more respect for a successor that understands the business as a whole.

Mesh with Retirement

Successor timing is inextricably linked with your own retirement goals and plans. Much of the timing has to do with the readiness of the successor and the state of the business climate, but a large minority is based on the owner's readiness. When you are determining your own readiness, it is important to avoid these four mistakes: transitioning all at once, transitioning before the successor is ready, transitioning too slowly, or staying too long.

The best way to avoid these errors is with a managed transition period in which control is given to the successor in a series of stair-steps. By implementing such a program, you avoid the risk of overwhelming your successor by giving him too much control, or frustrating him with not enough control; plus, it gives you the side benefit of helping yourself adjust to your new-found freedom and mobility.

Remember, an owner is absolutely entitled to retaining ownership until he dies (it is his company after all), but owning and running a business are two different things. I have worked with too many owners that still showed up to the shop every day to run operations well into their 80s. It is inadvisable to maintain tight control at that age; it cripples your successor and hog-ties your business.

Contingency Planning

As humans, we simply cannot control everything. You may have the best transition plan ever, but the problem is that things seldom go exactly to plan. Due to incapacity or death, your successor may have to take over sooner than you planned. Several key employees may leave or technology may change your business model. Whatever the case, it is vital to have contingency plans in place.

Too often, owners think that they, and their companies, are invulnerable. The problem with that mentality is that it blinds people to risk. Make sure you have accurately assessed the risks and have accounted for them. Just this year, one of my friends died of a heart attack in his early 60s. Today, his son runs a business he didn't think he would run for ten to fifteen years. In life, you just never know. Be prepared for the unthinkable.

There really is no perfect formula for timing a transition, or for creating a succession plan. Every business is different, but the key to success in any situation is to accommodate opportunity and manage risk. You simply must understand your own family situation and the business environment around you.

If you have multiple potential successors, you might have to take them through a series of tests or trial periods to see if a clear winner emerges. You may have to give them different positions and let them share power.

I even know of some families who have spun off different segments of their main business into standalone side businesses that each child now runs. Whatever your situation warrants, I hope you recognize that the sooner you start to plan, the better.

CHAPTER 9

Sale to Employees

Athens, Greece, 356 B.C.–323 B.C.

The man Alexander seems to belong more to legend than history. He tore through the ancient world like a meteor. Many historians rank him as one of the most influential men of all time. His presence was so keenly felt that he left behind a brand new civilization in his wake. Alexander's Greek colonists spread Greek thought and culture throughout the known world, mixing it with Eastern ideas and culture. This hybridization of East and West resulted in the Hellenistic culture, which survived well into the Byzantine Empire, more than a thousand years later.

At only the tender age of sixteen, Alexander the Great began the military career that would consume the rest of his life. His first victory came with the subjugation of revolting Thracians, but he quickly went on to help his father conquer all of Greece. With the death of his father, Alexander set out to conquer the Persian Empire at the age of twenty. At first the Persians ignored Alexander, but that proved to be a fatal mistake. After a series of losses, the Persian King Darius took personal command of his army and faced Alexander at the Battle of Issus. Alexander led his elite cavalry personally, breaking through the Persian flanks and then attacking Darius directly. Despite being outnumbered two to one, Alexander crushed the Persian center. When Darius fled, his entire army followed suit or surrendered. Issus was a pivotal point in the war, for it was the first time a Persian army had ever been defeated with the king on the field of battle.

The fall of Tyre and Gaza and victory at the battle of Gaugamela quickly followed on the heels of Issus. With the death of Darius shortly thereafter, the entire Persian Empire fell to Alexander's hands. Despite his success, Alexander was not content. His ambition could not be sated and he pushed into India, ever seeking the edges of the world. It was in India that his men finally mutinied, refusing to go any further. Alexander reluctantly agreed to turn back when the men refused to be persuaded by entreaties and speeches. He was said to have lost nearly three-fourths of his army to the harsh desert heat on the march home.

With his return from Asia, Alexander found his empire in shambles. He executed several of his military governors in an attempt to restore order and quell discontent. He was even forced to negotiate with his troops, the very ones who used to worship him as a hero, because they were angry at his adoption of Persian culture. Alexander had plans to conquer Saudi Arabia as well as Central Asia, but he never saw his projects come to fruition. At the age of thirty-two, Alexander died of some kind of sickness, possibly a fever.

Alexander the Great was perhaps the most successful military commander in the history of the planet. Tutored by one of the greatest minds the world has ever seen, raised by a mighty king, given command of a battle-hardened army, and driven by an internal fire unparalleled by mortal men, Alexander had every element necessary for success. He overthrew the most powerful empire in existence. He was undefeated in battle. For ten straight years he never lost a fight. It was his utmost wish to reach the ends of the world and the great outer sea. His empire reached from Greece to Egypt and east all the way to India.

Alexander truly was great. Yet for all his greatness, his empire died with him. At his death, his four top generals divided the empire between them and headed their separate ways. Alexander's belief in his own immortality caused him to disregard succession planning. He had no obvious or legitimate heir available to take over and he had no plans to transition control of his empire. According to legend, when Alexander was asked on his deathbed to whom he bequeathed his kingdom, he replied, "To the strongest." Alexander's lack of a plan touched off forty years of civil war that resulted in the murder of his family and closest friends.

The reason why many owners miss opportunities at the most vital point of their careers (i.e. their exit) is because they enjoy the idea of planning, but they refuse to change anything. For better or worse, owners tend to be dominant personalities. It allows them to be effective leaders and get things done, but it also gets in the way of a successful exit.

When selling or transitioning to an insider, pre-sale planning is just as vital as it would be for an outside sale. Even if the transition simply involves gifting or leaving the business to an heir, a serious amount of work needs to be done to make it a smooth transition. You will need to conduct an evaluation of cash flow and value, structure key employee buy-in, determine the final purchase value, and then decide the final exit path.

The insider exit path becomes the choice for transition when your children don't want to run the business, or are not equipped to, and you have a dedicated, loyal employee that has been with you for years. Insider transactions often involve rewarding a long-time and loyal employee, but at the same time extracting value from the business for your own family and retirement.

Remember that no matter how your transition is structured, it will still be failure if it doesn't accomplish these three primary objectives.

- Transfer to whom you want

- Transfer when you want

- Transfer for the price you need or desire

The question is, how do you attain those objectives when any insider to whom you will sell is not likely to have the significant amount of cash it will take to buy you out? No bank in its right mind would lend that kind of money to an insider without an enormous amount of collateral. Since it is unlikely that any insider will have the money to buy the business outright, the cash that he will need has to come from the business. After all, it is the business that pays your key employees. It is unlikely that they have a significant source of wealth from somewhere else; otherwise they probably wouldn't be working for you.

Because of the challenges inherent in an insider transition, such as cash flow and risk, you will need to follow the tried and true process for effective insider transitions. The first step is to have the new owners replace you in the business operations. It doesn't mean you just hand over the reins and then ride off into the sunset, but it does mean you will need to slowly transition out of leadership. It needs to become the responsibility of the proposed new owners to run the business, or at least create a team that will.

The next step involves slowly transferring ownership interest without losing control. You can do this a number of ways including: a small gift of stock or a sale of a minority interest with the promise to sell the balance once your objectives are met, or the certainty of being met is guaranteed. You should establish objective standards for your potential successor to meet before the ownership is sold, objectives such as receipt of purchase money, release of your personal liability exposure, pay off of business debt, and etc.

After the appropriate time period and standards are met, begin transferring a majority of the equity ownership through nonvoting stock or similar types of ownership interest that allows you to maintain control through owning a majority of the voting interest. This allows you to transfer more than 50 percent of the equity without risking ownership control.

Remember, no matter what transfer method you use, no matter how closely you watch the transfer, no matter how much you trust your employees or co-owners, it is vital that you always have a buy-back agreement which allows you to reacquire all of the transferred ownership upon the occurrence of certain events, such as: default in making payments to you when due, default in making payments to third-party lenders, a decrease in the net equity of the business, or any other measures or standards you deem vital to the best interest of the business.

The final step is to transfer control when, and only when, all of your ownership objectives have been met. You can structure the transfer a number of different ways, but in this chapter I'm going to cover only the four most effective. You can use them in concert, or individually.

Before we get to the specific strategies, you have to understand that a transfer to an insider other than your own children is going to have its own host of issues and complexities that you will have to confront. Regardless of the transfer method chosen, you will need to address these two fundamental questions:

- How do I minimize tax consequences to the business, to the new owner, and to me on the transfer of my business?

- How do I structure the transaction to guarantee I receive all the monies due me?

Tax is going to be an issue that will chase you around life no matter where you go. In fact, Uncle Sam is so benevolent that even if you are an American citizen living overseas and you make all your money in a foreign land, you will still be afforded the infinite pleasure of paying U.S. taxes. Isn't that so kind of our government, making sure we pay our tax bill from anywhere on the planet?

But even before you jump into tax issues, you have to assess the readiness of your insiders. Be careful about presuming that insiders actually want to buy your business. In July of 2013, we were hired to plan for what was supposed an insider sale for a fertilizer and chemical company. The owner, Charlie, intended to have his long-time employee, Fernando, buy the company. After our first few months of work, it was time to sit down with Fernando to explore how the transition might work.

However, when we introduced the plan to Fernando, he said, "Thank you so much for this opportunity and the trust you have in me to make this offer. However, I intend to retire and go back to Mexico to be with my family." Turns out Fernando had been investing his money into a nice place for him and his wife to retire near his family in Mexico. Now it was time for Charlie to pivot and look for another option for his transition planning.

Sometimes your transition plan will encounter unexpected twists, which it is why it is so important to lay the groundwork well in advance so that no matter what happens you will be prepared. When you deal with an inside transition, you may begin to transfer ownership only to have to buy it back because of missed objectives, or you may have to switch tactics due to changing circumstances. No matter what happens though, the key to an insider transfer is to structure the deal in such a way that the tax consequences are minimized for everyone involved, and your rights to cash flow are protected. There are a variety of strategies used to transfer ownership, but the most common and effective are these four:

- Sale of Stock

- Nonqualified Deferred Compensation

- Enhanced Qualified Retirement Plan Contributions

- Employee Stock Ownership Plan

We will dive into each of these tactics in further detail in just a minute, but first we need to remember that in an insider transition, 100 percent of the cash needed to purchase the initial buy-in of the insiders generally must come from the business. Unfortunately, there is an inherent problem. You own the business and therefore you own the cash flows. If you use current cash flow to fund your transition, you are essentially buying yourself out and giving away your company for free.

So only when some of the cash flows belong to someone else will you receive your due reward. This creates a few problems, but also a host of opportunities. Problem number one is that it creates risk. We know that the sooner you get your cash, the less risk you have. By deferring your payment over a number of years, you increase the odds that you will not receive full payment. After all, if the business is funding your buyout and the business goes under after you leave, you will be up a creek without a paddle.

We will address ways to combat your increased risk from an insider transition, but first let's dive into each of the four strategies. One or a combination of these strategies may be used to create a successful exit for you, while minimizing the risks you face in a sale to an insider.

Sale of Stock

When you sell your stock, you will have to pay capital gains tax on the difference between the price you sell for and your basis in the stock. If you are not familiar with basis, an easy way to think of it is simply the price you originally paid for your stock. Being the fair and judicious organization that it is, the IRS doesn't want to tax you on the same money twice, so they exclude money that you are simply receiving back and only tax you on the gain. If you are the owner of a closely-held business, chances are your basis is going to be incredibly low compared to your final selling price, so you will have to pay capital gains tax on the vast majority of your proceeds.

At first glance, a capital gains tax on your proceeds doesn't sound so bad. After all, the long-term capital gains rate is only 15 percent (or 20 percent if you are in the highest personal tax bracket, currently 39.5 percent), but remember what we said about double taxation. If you sell C Corp stock to employees, the money will go through that whole process that looks something like this:

- Dollar is earned by business

- Business pays dollar to key employee

- Employee pays 35 percent on the dollar (FICA, state and federal income tax, Medicaid tax, etc.)

- Employee pays you the 65 cents he has left

- You pay 25 percent on the 65 cents

- Which leaves you with a total 49 cents on the dollar from the beginning of the payment

Depending on the current tax regime and what state you live in, that 49 cents could be a larger number or even smaller. Think about that. If you structure your buy-out the wrong way, the IRS may make more on the transaction than you will! That should not be. It is unjust for you to work your tail off for an entire career only to have the government sit on their hands doing nothing and make more than you on the sale of your business. It is your money, and you should take home as much of it as you possibly can.

Suffice it to say that the tax issue is a large one for the seller. Now, I bet at this point you are thinking, "Saving taxes is great and all, but I still need to get paid!" The key is to get the income you deserve without subjecting the business cash flow to a double tax, if possible. If you can structure the deal so that the cash flow is only taxed once, there will be more cash available to pay you. Not only will it make you more money, but you will also get to keep more. There are a few things you can do to reduce the tax consequences of a stock sale to an insider.

First, with enough of a window for the exit plan, if you have a C-Corp with less than 100 shareholders, you can generally file an S-election. Once that is filed, you can sell a 10-30 percent of the company to the insider, who will receive dividends, taxed to him, but deductible to the corporation. With those dividends, he can pay you for the stock he is buying. You can also build in protections for you in the event things do not work out in this new direction so that you can buy back the shares if necessary.

Once the employee has paid off the shares and satisfied other criteria you have set forth for him to reach during the interim, if he or she has enough equity, they may be able to go to a bank and borrow the funds necessary to buy out the rest of your stock. The more equity they have, the higher the likelihood of getting a bank loan.

Since you also want to reduce risk in the sale of the stock, diversify your retirement strategy, and still make the transaction possible, it is important to employ multiple strategies to reduce the value of the stock, but increase your net worth in other ways.

The lower the price your employees pay for your stock, the less money is subject to the double taxation of the government. That is, the employee earns money or receives dividends on which he pays tax. Then he pays you for the stock and you pay a capital gains tax on the amount of the gain on sale over basis. So we want to make the company worth less for the purpose of the sale, but provide you with value from the company in other ways to reach your goals.

Section 1202 Stock

Given that most of the businesses I work with are in the $5-$50 million range, a Section 1202 election is often a very pertinent strategy for my clients selling stock. If you are a C Corporation for tax purposes, Section 1202 of the Internal Revenue Code is a convenient exclusion. It was set up by Congress to incentivize investment in small business, which can save business owners a huge amount of money. It states that taxpayers (other than corporations) can exclude from gross income at least 50 percent of the gain recognized on the sale or exchange of qualified small business stock that is held for more than five years.

Depending on the business, the exclusion can go up even to 100 percent. For qualifying stock acquired after Feb. 17, 2009, and on or before Sept. 27, 2010, the exclusion percentage is 75 percent; for qualifying stock acquired after Sept. 27, 2010, and before Jan. 1, 2014, the exclusion percentage is 100 percent.

The definition of a qualifying small business, according to the IRS, is a subchapter C corporation that is worth less than $50 million. The stock also has to be acquired at original issue and be held for more than five years. Remember though, these limitations are merely the broad standards that must be met. The IRS has a host of other small hurdles that have to be cleared before a business qualifies for a Section 1202 exclusion.[37i]

Now, the exclusion does have some limitations. As it goes with any tax considerations, it is paramount that you work with your tax counsel before making any moves. The above paragraphs are not meant to be taken as individual tax advice. I merely want to make you aware of a strategy that may not have shown up on your radar before now. Even if Section 1202 is not relevant to your situation, we will turn to consider ways to reduce your risk in the sale of the business and also to make sure you or your family get paid, even on your death. One way is to enter into a deferred compensation agreement with your business well before you begin the sale transaction.

Deferred Compensation

Deferred compensation is a nice strategy because, even though it ends up having a similar tax consequence for you at the ownership level, it benefits the business. The business gets to deduct the deferred compensation paid out to you. Instead of needing to earn $1.60 to pay you a dollar, the business will only need to earn a single dollar to pay you one dollar.

The downside to deferred compensation is that, in order for it to work properly, the plan must be in place long before the actual sale event. The long timeframe needed to pull off deferred compensation well is just one more reason to start the BraveHeart Planning Process™ as early as possible.

A deferred compensation plan is a non-qualified pension plan and can be provided for any owner or key employee. It is essentially an agreement in which a portion of an employee's income is paid out at a later time than which the income was earned. A typical plan would pay out an agreed annual retirement benefit at age sixty-five for ten years. Some of what you would pay to the employee is invested in a life insurance policy and if sufficiently funded, the company borrows the annual amount against the policy to make the payments. Then with the balance of the value of the insurance, the policy is maintained by the company until your death. The company receives the death benefit and gets some or all of the money invested in the insurance policy back as insurance proceeds. These work better the younger you are when you take out the policies.

In addition to using deferred compensation, there are a number of other methods to help facilitate an insider buyout. These include:

- Lease payments

- Consulting fees

- Licensing fees

- Royalties

Having the owner, who many times owns the land on which the business operates, enter into a lease with the company for the highest defensible amount possible is a great way to extract value from your business and reduce its value. Long-term contracts or debt reduce net income for a company and thus reduce its value to a buyer. That makes it cheaper and easier to sell and reduces long-term capital gains taxes to the seller.

If your business is capital intensive, you could buy the equipment personally (or better yet, buy it with a limited liability entity owned by you) and then turn around and lease it back to the business, again burdening the company with payments, and thus reducing its value. After the equipment is paid off, rental payments continue, which give you a tax-deductible method of receiving value for the business after you have left. Plus, the equipment is secured and not subject to claims by the creditors of the business because you own it, not the business.

You may also enter into a consulting contract for the company that will remain in place after you sell the company. Much like deferred compensation, these fees are tax deductible to the business and treated as ordinary income for you. You will have to provide services for the income, but that does not generally require as much time as being a full-time employee.

There may be other opportunities, depending on whether you own patents or technology outside your company, which you could license or for which you could charge royalties. This, of course, requires you to have something that can be licensed, such as an idea, copyright, or patent. However, if you do have any of these, keeping them out of the business will allow you to receive deductible payments.

The key to each of these strategies is that you charge a fee that is both high and defensible. You do not want the IRS coming after you, but you also don't want to pay them any more than you absolutely have to pay. As with anything in business, and life for that matter, it is a balance. These techniques are great strategies that benefit the business and the owner, but you still have to be careful that you can defend the deductions and payouts.

Also, remember to take a sufficient amount of money out of the business as you go along. Too many owners accumulate too much money inside of the business by constantly underpaying themselves and reinvesting into the business. Waiting till the end to get your money out can create a burden when it comes time to transfer, especially in C corporations. The IRS may consider it "unreasonable compensation" and tax it at the company level as a dividend (which is not deductible by the business) and a taxable event for you. In addition, any excess cash that is inside the business is vulnerable to business creditors.

Increased Retirement Funding

Another great strategy is to use your retirement fund to reduce the value of the business and thus power your buyout. Contributions to retirement plans are tax deductible for the business, plus the tax on income earned through the plan is deferred until you withdraw the money from the plan. Usually, the plan cannot discriminate in your favor as the owner, which means that any funding for your benefit would also have to benefit every single participating employee. But as always, there are ways to work around the requirements.

With the proper design, you may be able to increase your own benefits relative to the retirement benefits of your employees or co-owners. Naturally, this will change the character and tax treatment of these payments, but not the total amount of the payment. If your company is set up so that you and the purchasers of your stock are the only significant participants in the retirement plan, it may be possible to have them (them being your key employees who are buying the company from you) opt out of the retirement plan. This will allow you to increase the funding formula so that a greater amount of the retirement benefits accumulate for you, but not for other younger participants. This way, you will receive a disproportionate amount of the company's cash flow as your retirement plan contribution.

Together the sum of these strategies can reduce the amount of money you will need to take out of the business at retirement. As with the deferred compensation strategy, retirement funding takes time and stops working once you leave, so keep that in mind as you consider them for retirement strategy.

ESOP

If you are not familiar with this method, ESOP stands for Employee Stock Ownership Plan. It is a profit sharing qualified plan that is adopted by an employer corporation. ESOPs are designed to invest primarily in the employer's stock, thus providing a place for the owner to sell the company. ESOPs differ in the ways they acquire and finance their corporation's stock, but each one ends up with stock in the employees' hands. The ESOP would own the stock pursuant to the purchase from the owner. Then, when an employee terminates his employment with the company he receives the portion of the stock, or its value in cash, that was allotted to him within the ESOP. Obviously, like any qualified plan, ESOPs have certain vesting and participation requirements.

ESOPs are a good strategy for owners of closely-held businesses that do not have a lot of exit options. They can also be a pivotal piece of a structured buy out by co-owners, employees, or third parties. The reason ESOPs are so widely used is that they allow owners of C corporations to sell their stock to the ESOP and thereby defer all gain on that sale, provided the proceeds are reinvested in publicly-traded stocks and bonds (interestingly enough, investment in mutual funds is not allowed).

Whatever you choose, whether ESOP or deferred compensation or other strategies, make sure you make your expectations and plans clear to your employee if you are planning on transitioning to an insider. What you intend as a gift may be taken as a burden. Employees come in all personalities and ambitions. You may have several employees that would jump at the chance to buy your business or you may have none. You might have one clear key employee or a group of them. Just like any other piece of the BraveHeart Process, the sooner you plan and make decisions, the better.

CHAPTER 10

Sale to Third Party

Paris, France, June 28, 1919

The evening sun sparkles through the room, reflected off row upon row of mirrors. Gilt carvings adorn walls that rise up to meet lofty ceilings. The Hall of Mirrors invokes a sense of splendor and majesty, a mood little matched by the defeated German commanders. Bristling with humiliated pride and national defeat, the generals of the once vaunted German Military read the agreement. Across from them sit the arrogant French, the inflexible English, and the untried Americans. The Germans tighten their fists in anger as they read Article 231:

"The Allied and Associated Governments affirm and Germany accepts the responsibility of Germany and her allies for causing all the loss and damage to which the Allied and Associated Governments and their nationals have been subjected as a consequence of the war imposed upon them by the aggression of Germany and her allies."

The Germans glare at their unyielding counterparts. Assuming complete guilt for the war is a difficult pill to swallow, especially since they were drawn into the war by their loyalty to the Austrio-Hungarian Empire, the same empire that was also forced into war by the Serbian assassination of their leader. Unfortunately, there is nothing the Germans can do. Their economy is in shambles, their military has been defeated, and four and a half years of warfare has devastated their country. The German commanders heave a sigh and affix their signatures to the bottom of The Treaty of Versailles, officially ending World War One.

Along with the infamous War Guilt Clause, the Germans were also forced to disarm, cede substantial territories to their enemies, pay massive war reparations, and stomach a host of other concessions. The Treaty of Versailles was a hodge-podge of competing and sometimes conflicting interests of the Allies. The French were chiefly concerned with protecting their exposed border with Germany, since most of the Western Front was fought there. The British were mainly concerned with their economic empire, and so focused on the economic effects of the treaty. The Americans, on the other hand, ambitiously intended to reshape the very fabric of Europe, putting forth the League of Nations and Wilson's 14-Point Plan. The result was a treaty that sought to incorporate the demands of all the Allied nations, demands foisted on a Germany already devastated by war.

With the signing of the Treaty of Versailles, it appeared that the Allies had won. They drove hard bargains, threatening to resume hostilities should the Germans refuse to sign the document as it was. They were able to extract large concessions from the Germans that included war reparations of 132 billion marks (which would be roughly $442 billion in today's dollars), a demilitarized Rhineland buffer zone between France and Germany, and control of former German territories by the League of Nations. It was the perfect coup de grace, or so the Allies thought.

The only problem was that the Allies forgot that negotiation is not always just about the money. Sometimes winning a bargain is no win at all. The Treaty of Versailles officially ended World War One, but at the same time it sowed the seeds of World War Two. The German people considered the treaty to be a national humiliation and they groaned under the harsh terms of the agreement. The necessity of paying back enormous reparations caused the Germans to devalue their currency, plunging the country into even deeper economic straits. It was this pain and suffering upon which Hitler capitalized, enabling him to seize total power. If the Allies had considered the long-term implications of the treaty, and not just the short-term financial wins, they may have avoided a Second World War altogether.

The same short-term focus is found in many business sales today. The papers are littered with stories of company mergers gone wrong—and that's just the ones that make the news! From clashing cultures to inflated valuations, acquisitions run into a thousand different problems, many of which have nothing to do with financials. Selling a business is no easy feat, especially when so much is riding on the outcome. It is a knife-edge, from which one can easily fall. Whether they fall to deal euphoria or deal fatigue, business owners often fail at this critical juncture in their careers.

Yet, for many owners, selling their business is the moment they have dreamed of for years. Plenty of people want to leave their business to their children, but there is still a large majority who are ready to cash out and move on. Whether you are tired of your current company and itching to start a new one, or you are ready to take some time off and go on that trip you've been promising your wife for years, selling to a third party is the right move for quite a few owners. Sometimes it is the only way to receive the cash flow that you need in the timeframe you require. Hopefully that isn't the case for you. Selling should be a choice that you make because you want to make it. The purpose of the BraveHeart Process is to put the control back into your hands so that you get to choose, based on your goals and desires, not something you are forced into doing because of financial constraints.

Though selling to a third party has the potential to be incredibly lucrative, it is also fraught with many challenges and dangers. Selling your company will probably be the most emotional thing you've done since getting married or having children. It is a tough process that will put you through the ringer. The stakes are high and the choices sometimes irreversible. With such a high potential for slip-ups and such grave consequences for mistakes, it is paramount that you have highly competent advisors to walk with you through the process. It is also incredibly important that you have an understanding of what a proper sale process looks like when it is done correctly. I want to give you a brief overview of a properly conducted sale by smart owners and skilled advisors.

There are a thousand and one books on selling your business, but one of my favorites is *Sell Your Business for an Outrageous Price* by Kevin M. Short. If you want to dig deeper than I can cover in one chapter, pick up Kevin's book. If you'd like a lighter read, check out *Built to Sell* by John Warrilow. It's an allegorical tale that follows an owner through his work of building a company that thrives without him.

Now that you've got some extra resources, let's jump into the sale process. Just like the overall BraveHeart Plan, selling your business takes preparation and hard work. The more you know and the more ready the business, the higher the price you will should be able to get for your business. Selling your business isn't like selling a house. You won't be able to throw a sign in the front yard and start receiving offers.

Andrew Carnegie was once approached by J.P. Morgan about selling his steel and railroad empire. Carnegie thought about it for a moment, did some calculations, and threw out a number. J.P. Morgan promptly agreed. As soon as the papers were drawn up and signed, Carnegie became the richest man in the world. Out of curiosity, Carnegie asked J.P. Morgan if he would have still bought the company if Carnegie had asked for another $100 million. J.P. Morgan replied that he would have doubled the sale price and still gotten a bargain. Now, I don't know how much an extra $100 million means to the richest man in the world, but how sad is it that the most successful man of his day did not even know the value of his own company? Whether you sell for a $100 million or a $100 thousand, I want you to sell for a price that your company is worth and a price that you can live with. To do that, you will need to walk through the following steps:

1. Analyze mergers and acquisitions cycle and interest rates

2. Assess company and owner for sale readiness

3. Presale due diligence

4. Identify competitive advantage

5. Identify potential buyers

6. Controlled auction

7. Sale documents

8. Closing

9. Adjusting post sale expectations

The M&A Cycle

The first thing you need to do before you even consider putting the wheels in motion on executing your sale is to analyze the external business environment that your company operates in, specifically the market for businesses similar in size and scope to your own. In finance, they talk quite a bit about "intrinsic value." While that intrinsic value is certainly a factor, at the end of the day your business is worth the price that you can get for it. Just like in any market, the price of a business is determined by both buyer and seller constraints.

Consider an example for a moment. If you were haggling with a vender in Istanbul over a Persian rug, what factors would come into play? First there is the amount of cash you have in your pocket. You won't be able to buy the rug if you simply do not have the money. The next factor to come into play is the quality of the rug itself. If it is silk, hand-woven, aesthetically-pleasing, and durable, it will command a higher price than if it were otherwise. The next issue is whether the seller can make a profit or not. He may be willing to take a loss on the product, depending on how desperate he is, but it is unlikely he will want to do that. The final determinant in the Persian rug price is simply what similar rugs are selling for in the market.

In the same way, the M&A market is subject to several factors that change and adjust every time another business is sold. The first factor the market is affected by is fluctuating interest rates. Low stable rates provide buyers with cheap borrowed funds to buy your business. The higher interest rates rise, the less willing they are to borrow funds and the less likely they are to take that higher risk to purchase your company. Along a similar vein, deal activity is directly impacted by the availability and pricing of financing. If buyers can't secure the funds to buy your business, then there is really nowhere to go from there.

The M&A market is also affected by the overall health of the economy. As enthusiasm rises and economic activities pick up, more buyers will be looking to expand through acquisitions. The stock market valuations of publically-owned companies must also be taken to account because the higher their values rise, the more likely it is they will use their stock to buy other companies. The final factor that will affect your final sale price is simply supply and demand.

Sale Readiness

Once you have examined the market, it is time to become introspective and assess your own readiness to sell. Since you have walked through the majority of the exit process already, this is going to be the easy part for you. You have already solidified your personal objectives: i.e. how much money you will need from the transaction, when you want to sell (which in this case, the time has now come), and the type of transition you would like to occur (for you this is going to be an outside third party sale). You have already established a well-reasoned value estimation for your business as well as your exit goals, strategy, family considerations, advisors, and value catalysts. At this point you will also need to factor in competitors, potential buyers, industry acquisition activity, and your own competitive advantage.

Your advisors will want to dive into the insights you have on your company's competitors: who they are, whether you have ever exploited their weaknesses, and if there is a competitor who, in your opinion, might be a buyer. It will also be helpful for your sale team to know how your company measures up to applicable industry standards.

Knowledge on potential buyers is incredibly valuable to your sale team. They will most likely ask you to list your competitors, vendors, and others outside the company whom you think would benefit from buying your business. The reason you will want to conduct this analysis is that strategic buyers, those who are looking to buy your business to augment their own, often pay the highest prices.

You will also want to share your expertise and knowledge about industry-specific valuation issues with your team. If you are familiar with the details of recent acquisitions, why buyers are making purchases, what form of payment they are using, how much they are paying out, and the size of the acquisitions they are going after, you will be able to anticipate the other side's negotiation tactics. This information will help you get zeroed in on the playing field you will be maneuvering in.

The final issue you need to dig out is your own company's competitive advantage. Do you know why customers buy from you instead of from your competitors? Have you thought about developing and verbalizing your competitive advantage? What about how to better position your company to appeal to buyers? Owners, who can clearly articulate just why their customers prefer their business, can have an enormous advantage at the bargaining table. Knowing exactly what makes your company better gives you a solid footing to negotiate for a superior price.

Presale Due Diligence

No matter the size of the transaction, due diligence is a part of every sale. As I've mentioned before, buyers hate risk. They will do everything they can to reduce risk and that includes burrowing into every single business record they can get their hands on. They are especially on the lookout for evidence of malfeasance or undisclosed material risk, such as fraud, on the part of the selling owner or his managers. They will look into everything that you want to hide, whether that is unpaid taxes, pending or threatened litigation, or technical obsolescence of your equipment, processes, products, or services. They will also want to find areas where they can make immediate improvements (and thereby earn more revenue) such as inefficiencies, waste, and mismanagement.

Due diligence is a daunting proposition for owners looking to sell. The process of collecting and organizing all the data needed is a demanding task. What makes it especially tough is that much of document gathering has to be conducted discreetly. Owners typically keep these matters confidential and only communicate the sale to the employees that are necessary to help prepare for and execute the sale. Even though most sellers understand the need for due diligence, that doesn't take away from the fact that it is an emotional and invasive procedure. Furthermore, not all buyers have honorable intentions. There are acquirers out there who have no intention of closing a deal, but instead conduct due diligence to steal information and gain a competitive advantage over the seller. Finally, due diligence is tough because it can be a big, long, and drawn-out process. The higher the purchase price you seek, the deeper and wider the due diligence your buyer will need to conduct.

To combat the emotional fatigue and the grueling workload associated with due diligence, you conduct internal presale due diligence. Think of it as a dress rehearsal. When I was in law school, I competed in moot court competitions. Before we would go to the actual competition, we would often have a pre-trial practice session in which we faced a team of our friends that would cross-examine us and try to poke holes in our case at every weak point they could find. After the exercise, we would come together and discuss ways to improve and shore up our weaknesses.

The same principle is at work in the presale due diligence. It helps give owners a small taste of what they will endure later so that they will be prepared when the time comes. Additionally, it's helpful for the owner to take a devil's advocate approach. If sellers can step back and look at their company like an outsider, it will help to align their expectations with reality. No buyer is going to walk into the negotiating room with a signed check in hand for a company he knows nothing about.

Buyers will do everything they can to depress the sale price. Due diligence is one of the many tools they use. You can expect that any inconsistency they find, any small weakness, will be exploited. Presale due diligence allows you the chance to spot these irregularities before the buyer does, so you can be prepared for negotiations. When it comes to negotiation, preparation is half the battle.

Competitive Advantage

Identifying your competitive advantage is critical because it is a foundational piece of the asking price. It allows you and your team to tell a compelling story, to not just sell your business but to sell it well. It allows you to sell your buyers on your company's true worth, as you understand it. By focusing on what makes your company valuable, you are sticking to what matters in the minds of buyers. You need to know what sets you apart from the pack before you head to market. Anyone who is not able to communicate this advantage puts himself at an immediate disadvantage when it comes to competing for buyers.

By way of review, a competitive advantage is any feature or features that allow you to make a product or offer a service either better or more cheaply than your competitors for a sustainable period of time. The best matchup is when your competitive advantage fits the buyer's need. According to Michael Porter, author of *Competitive Advantage: Creating and Sustaining Superior Performance,* it is paramount to develop and nurture a competitive advantage in order to not only maintain but also improve your company's financial performance.

Porter states, "Competitive advantage grows fundamentally out of value a firm is able to create for its buyers that exceeds the firm's cost of creating it. Value is what buyers are willing to pay, and super value stems from offering lower prices than competitors for equivalent benefits or providing unique benefits that more than offset a higher price. There are two basic types of competitive advantage: cost leadership and differentiation."[xxxix]

The concept of competitive advantage is closely tied to saleability. Not all companies have the ability to be sold. When buyers are looking for acquisitions, they hunt for companies that have a long profitable history. They are looking for companies in a stable or growing industry. Buyers want to acquire companies that have employees with special skills or expertise, a competent management team, a motivated workforce, and above all, they want companies that will provide them an acceptable return on their investment.

Potential Buyers

When it comes to selling a business, there are two primary types of buyers: financial and strategic.

Financial buyers acquire firms based on a financial formula. They use this formula to determine the price they are willing to pay for acquisitions. The key component of the buying formula is the required rate of return. A classic example of a financial buyer is a private equity group.

Financial buyers often buy businesses in industries with which they are not intimately acquainted. This means that sellers will spend more time educating them during the due diligence process. Generally, financial buyers are looking toward the exit even as they buy. Pulling the trigger for these buyers depends solely on the opportunity to inject capital into a business they can turn around and sell for a profit within a reasonable timeframe.

Strategic buyers, on the other hand, base their purchase price offer on their perception of your company's future value to them. Acquisitions are often made to augment their existing holdings; as a result, they look for synergies between their current operations and yours. They look to leverage their own market distribution, name recognition, or proprietary technology and outperform what you could have done on your own.

There are four primary types of strategic buyers: competitors, verticals, industry players, and adjacencies. The easiest place to look for potential buyers is of course competitors. Your advisors will typically look to see if one or more of your competitors would benefit from acquiring your company. The reason competitors usually buy each other out is to increase market share or to eliminate a competitor. Though competitors are a good place to start, discretion is necessary. You and your advisors should discreetly evaluate the risks associated with dealing with each competitor. You should generally stay away from those in your industry with bad reputations, even if they happen to be larger and capable of buying your company. Sometimes these competitors can do you damage with just the knowledge that you are looking to sell.

Another good place to look for buyers is upstream or downstream on the supply chain. Your advisors should scan the pool for suppliers or purchasers who could benefit by diversifying vertically rather than horizontally. If your company is a major customer of one of its suppliers, it may interest that supplier to secure a big account by buying it out. Cutting out the middleman has always been a classic cost saver in any industry. Moving vertically, a major customer might want to buy your firm in order to manage costs for critical or costly components. Your firm represents just one more variable that could be eliminated when taking into account the cost of goods sold.

An industry player is a business that is engaged in the same activity as you, but is not a direct competitor. Many times this is due to diversity in geographic areas. Industry players sometimes pay a premium for the ability to expand their territory, acquire customers, or eliminate overhead.

Adjacencies are the least obvious of the potential buyers and therefore require the most research to find. They are businesses that complement your business, but don't directly operate in your industry. For instance, an electrical supply company may be interested in acquiring a plumbing supply company to expand its customer base and product offering. Adjacencies are a nice alternative to competitors because they do not know your industry and your information is not as dangerous in their hands.

Once you have identified all the potential buyers in your network, area, supply chain, and circles, your team will begin to gather intelligence on them. Your advisors will look into their past acquisitions, prices paid, changes in strategic acquisitions plans, problems they may be encountering, changes in industry position or reputation, personnel changes, or changes in the regulatory environment.

Controlled Auction

Once you have conducted all the presale preparations, you are ready to execute. The question is then, what format is most appropriate for your context? The two main options are a competitive auction (sometimes called a controlled auction) and a negotiated sale. As the name implies, in a competitive auction, multiple qualified buyers bid simultaneously to purchase a company. In an auction, the buyers negotiate not only with the seller but also against each other. A negotiated sale, on the other hand, involves only two parties: the buyer and the seller. In my experience, a competitive auction is the superior method to selling a company because the negotiated sale tilts the scales in favor of the buyer getting a higher price for the company.

Most people end up in a negotiated sale, not because they necessarily want to be there but because they are trapped there. What ends up happening is that the seller receives an offer from a qualified potential buyer that he may or may not have expected. From there, he wants to get the best price he possibly can, so he enlists the aid of an investment banker, lawyer, or CPA, not to structure the deal but to help him in the negotiation process. The problem is that the seller has handicapped himself from the start. Skilled buyers know that to pull out of a negotiated sale is very difficult so you will be reluctant to walk away. If you cannot maintain walk away power, your leverage has been completely taken away.

A controlled auction comes with a variety of benefits. It will give you an enormous leg up by forcing the buyers to compete against each other. Competition forces them to pay more for your business than they otherwise would have. You know this principle firsthand. I think we have all overpaid for items that we bought at an auction or on eBay. Furthermore, an auction allows the seller to consider several different offers in order to pick the one that best meets his objectives, both financial and otherwise.

The auction allows you to release information in a controlled manner, so that you stay in charge, not the buyer. Not only are you in charge of information flow but you also gain negotiating strength on every other deal point from purchase price and timing to the extent of due diligence. With a controlled auction, your eggs are spread out among several baskets. You have less risk if the deal doesn't close, which maintains your vital walk away power. Finally, with an auction, your advisors will be able to bring to the table buyers that you hadn't even thought about. Overall, a controlled auction is the smart way to sell your business.

Sale Documents

Every sale is going to come with a host of documents, some more important than others. Understanding what each is intended for, as well as their strengths and limitations, will aid you in your negotiation. Once again, I can't stress enough how important it is to have an experienced deal team. Documents often hide ticking time bombs, which have the potential to blow up in your face even after all the papers are signed. It is vital that you understand the terms of your agreements. Having advisors who know what they are doing will help you know what is customary in a sale process and what you should not have to put up with. The most important documents in a sale process are:

- The Confidentiality Agreement

- The Letter of Intent

- The Term Sheet

- The Definitive Purchase Agreement

Confidentiality Agreement

Every sale will include a confidentiality agreement, but not all of them are the same. The confidentiality agreement is a legally-binding document, the contents of which are subject to negotiation. The primary purpose of the agreement is to protect your business from unauthorized disclosure or use of confidential information provided by you to the potential buyer. If your customers or key employees catch wind too quickly that you are selling, it could be disastrous. This agreement is typically drafted by your own attorney. Protecting your intellectual property and trade secrets during the sale process is absolutely vital.

Letter of Intent

The letter of intent will also be in the beginning stages of selling your business. It *should* be a non-binding agreement that describes the business terms of the contemplated transaction and begins to set forth certain contingencies. Some of these contingencies can be financial, such as the ability of the buyer to obtain financing. The contingencies can also be legal in nature, such that the deal will only close on satisfactory completion of due diligence or agreement by all necessary parties.

In short, the letter of intent outlines the terms of the deal. It is your attorney's job to ensure that the letter of intent stays non-binding; however, there is one item that buyers will tend to insist on, and that is your agreement to take the business off the market for a limited time, usually ninety to one hundred and twenty days, while you agree to negotiate only with a single buyer.

Term Sheet

The term sheet is created to outline what the buyer will actually be purchasing. There are two basic ways to buy a business. You can either buy its stock or its assets. A stock purchase involves the agreement to buy the equity of a company for a defined price, and the agreement of the buyer to assume all the seller's liabilities. Smaller deals tend to be structured as asset purchases because buyers want to avoid hidden liabilities and they want to have the ability to depreciate assets in order to get a tax advantage for their purchase.

The term sheet also outlines the purchase price or, as is the more common method in business sales, the purchase price calculation. Usually, the parties agree on a formula that details how the purchase price will be computed. All of the items on the term sheet are subject to negotiation. The term sheet details any earn-out period, escrow or holdback of funds, assumed liabilities, breakup fees, operating restrictions, employment agreements, covenants not to compete, anticipated closing date, and much more. Each of these agreements has the potential to have a huge impact on your bottom line and your post-exit lifestyle. Getting the term sheet right is critical.

Definitive Purchase Agreement

This is the document that will embody the all the terms and conditions of the agreement for the sale of the company. Everything about the deal has to be included in this document. This agreement contains the conditions that must be satisfied before there is an obligation to complete the transaction, like licenses or regulatory approvals. It will also contain the representations and warranties by the seller, which must be true at the time of closing, or there could be penalties or refunds and it could end in litigation. It will also include covenants, which will control conduct of the parties, both before and after closing of the sale. This could include restrictions on operations of the company after signing but before closing, as an example.

This is where the skill of your lawyer comes into play. He or she will negotiate to minimize the representations and warranties you are required to make, work to minimize risk to you in the deal and to maximize what you keep. There are many, many deal points to negotiate. The definitive purchase agreement tends to be seventy to one hundred pages long. You will need to know your lawyer is skilled in this work or find another.

The supporting schedules to the contract are also a very, very important part of the document, as these are the things that ultimately spell out what the buyer is buying. Failure to adequately or accurately disclose the things that the supporting schedules call for can give rise to significant risks, purchase price adjustments, or litigation.

Closing

The penultimate step has finally come. In the closing stage, you will work through the buyer's performance of final due diligence, the negotiation of financing contingencies, and the negotiation of the definitive purchase agreement, as well as some other transaction documents. It is imperative that you do not let down your guard at this stage. The transaction is far from over. Closing involves the most crucial moments of the entire deal. Remember that nothing is over until all your money is in the bank, which can happen six months to several years *after* the closing date. By the time you close, you are almost done, but not quite, so be prepared to keep up the momentum and the pressure on the deal.

We managed the sale of a real estate company in the southeastern part of the country for Harry. We picked an M&A firm to represent the company and hired a law firm to handle the sales contract and some of the negotiation process. We spent eight months on preparation, marketing, and squeezing the potential buyers down to one. We went into sixty days of due diligence with a private equity buyer. The winning offer was $1 million dollars above the rest of the offers. Everything went wonderfully... until a few days before we were supposed to close.

The buyer, a private equity firm, all of a sudden claimed that we had not disclosed that two of the clients of the seller's company were merging and thus would reduce the amount of income earned by the company thereafter. This was a complete fabrication. I was in the meetings with the private equity buyer and know that it was both disclosed orally and was included in the projections of the business income for the next year. We pointed these things out to the buyer in the numbers ourselves. It was totally accounted for and disclosed. Yet, the buyer claimed it did not know that and was pulling out of the sale.

The buyer resubmitted their offer to buy a few days later, but reduced by 20 percent. Harry refused to walk away from this company and their manipulation of the truth, because he wanted to sell. He made a small counter offer and the deal closed. That is called a "cram down." It is one of a number of tactics buyers use to squeeze down the price they pay the seller. They are looking for any small reason possible to justify the opportunity to pull one over on you. The tactic takes advantage of deal fatigue and fear. The seller does not want to risk having to go back to the other potential buyers that were passed over, for they fear they will not still be willing to buy or they will also reduce their price. The seller is also at the point where they just want to be done. I find these tactics more effective on deals less than $50 million or so, because those smaller deals are more likely sellers who are a little less sophisticated and probably going through their first sale.

The whole point of running your business full tilt down to the very end of the process is that it allows you to emotionally and financially say no to an overreaching buyer or untenable adjustment just before the closing transaction. It is vital that you maintain your walk away power until the funds hit the bank. By being careful not to get psychologically and emotionally tied to the deal, you could make literally millions of dollars extra on the sale.

Cram downs are not the only things you need to watch carefully. You must also make sure that you devote the energy you need to run your business while you are going through this process. Remember that buying formula we talked about? Maintaining the sale price you desire will often depend on how your business performs during the sale process. Some big components of the sale formula include things like working capital and demonstrated growth patterns. Your business needs to kick into overdrive during this process so that you can finish out strong, in order to obtain the price you want.

The final price will be subject to a price adjustment based on the buyer's post-closing audit of items on your balance sheet such as net worth, working capital and accounts receivable. Your books will be reviewed by the buyer at the end of the transaction because business value is a fluid asset. Inventories, cash on hand, and accounts receivable fluctuate on a daily basis. If you put in the work during the presale due diligence, keep your momentum in the business up, and negotiate well, these post-closing adjustments should be relatively minor. The reason we emphasize preparation is that it comes in handy at this stage. We want to avoid a significant negative price adjustment right at the end of the process.

After you close, it may take twelve to thirty-six months to wrap up all the longer-term issues such as the release of escrow funds, indemnification, survival period, payments on holdback notes, and any earn outs.

Post Sale Expectations

You've done it! You've sold your business. Congratulations! Let it sink in for a moment. But don't believe that's the last step in life!

Before you get to the finish line, envision your life after you cross it. If you only focus on your last days in business and never stop and think about what it will be like after a sale, you may well be disappointed when your business finally does sell. Don't worry if it is a scary thought to think about what you will do post-business! Plenty of owners have wondered if life after the sale could be as satisfying, challenging, and as fulfilling as life as an owner.

It can be a paralyzing place to be, but it doesn't have to be. You can make sound decisions for your life and your company, you just have to discover what you want and then make your goals explicit. Anything new in life is scary. As human beings we do not like change, but unfortunately change is inevitable. I like to tell my clients, "The only thing in life that doesn't change is that everything changes." Selling or transitioning your business is just one more stage in life to which you must adjust. Like everything in the Exit Process, proper preparation is vital. Visualizing what you want and then taking the steps to get there is the key to having a satisfying life post-exit.

CHAPTER 11

Life after Transition

Jerusalem, Israel, 848 B.C.–796 B.C.

A young king stares up at the ceiling, unable to sleep. Though the crown lies on a table by his bedside, he can still feel its weight upon his brow. "By all rights, I should be content," he tries to tell himself. His power base is secure, the people have crowned him king, and his enemies are powerless to oppose him, yet still the sleep flees from his eyes. A soft breeze flutters the curtains, whispering peace and stillness, but Solomon feels none of it. He finally rises up and walks across the room, ducking through the long drapes at his window. He steps onto the balcony beyond. Beneath him, Jerusalem lays spread. A full moon illuminates a thousand rooftops, as far as the eye can see. Solomon leans over the rail and puts his head down. Shutting his eyes, he can almost feel the voice of the nation. All is still, but in the morning they will come, clamoring for justice, complaining of taxes, crying with suffering. They will come to him, yearning for him to speak, to solve their problems.

Solomon lifts his head again, wishing his father were with him. "The City of David they call it, but now David is gone," Solomon whispers softly to himself. He turns from the balcony and picks up his father's crown, fingering the intricate design. Eventually Solomon sets the crown aside and lies down, wondering how he will be able to live up to his father's legacy. He falls asleep with little idea how quickly he will get the chance.

The very next day, two women come to him with a dispute for him to judge. Solomon listens intently as the first woman states her case. "O my lord, this woman and I live in the same house," she says, pointing accusingly at the

*other woman. "This woman's son died in the night, because she lay on him.
So she rose in the middle of the night and took my son from my side, while
I slept, and laid him in her bosom, and laid her dead child in my bosom.
And when I rose in the morning to nurse my son, there he was—dead. But
when I had examined him in the morning, indeed, he was not my son whom
I had borne."*

*The other woman jumps in, cutting her off. "No! But the living one is my
son, and the dead one is your son."*

*The first woman quickly fires back, "No! But the dead one is your son, and
the living one is my son."*

*Solomon strokes his beard for a moment and then shrugs. "Bring me a sword!"
he demands. "Divide the living child in two, and give half to one, and half
to the other," he proclaims nonchalantly. The true mother of the child gasps
and says , "O my lord, give her the living child, and by no means kill him!"*

But the other said, "Let him be neither mine nor yours, but divide him."

*Solomon leans back and smiles. Standing up he proclaims his verdict. "Give
the first woman the living child, and by no means kill him; she is his mother."*

*When all Israel heard of the judgment which the king had rendered, they
feared the king, for they saw that the wisdom of God was in him to administer
justice.*

*The days of Solomon brought an unparalleled period of peace and prosperity.
The Book of Kings says that silver became as common as paving stones and
cedar as common as sycamore trees. Solomon's traders bought horses from
Egypt, spices from Arabia, monkeys from Africa, dye from the Phoenicians,
cedar from Tyre, and every other kind of good from all over the known world.
Solomon's wisdom and wealth became so famous that the Queen of Sheba
came hundreds of miles just to hear him speak. When she got to Jerusalem,
she decided the stories didn't do his wisdom or his kingdom half the justice
they deserved.*

While Solomon may have enjoyed the days of peace, it was his father who
created them. David was a hard man and a soldier all the days of his life.
He tirelessly fought to turn the nation of Israel from a loosely organized
band of independent tribes into a unified kingdom and a regional

powerhouse. David always dreamed of building a temple, but it was not to be in his lifetime. Instead he amassed natural resources beyond count so that his son Solomon could carry on his life's work. It took Solomon seven years to build the temple and thirteen years to build his own palace, but by the end of the work, Solomon's constructions surpassed even the palaces of much larger nations. The nation of Israel lived in a golden age all the years of Solomon's life because his father David was willing to work on a dream that wouldn't see fulfillment until after his death.

Many business owners live for the day they can finally sell their business, or pass it off to a worthy heir. Unfortunately, many owners don't realize that what happens after the sale may be far more important to their financial and emotional well-being than the actual sale. Post sale is where many owners go awry and it is such a shame because it is the season of life that should be the sweetest. Owners often dream of the day that they can go at a little slower pace; when they can relax, spend time with their families, and enjoy the little things in life.

> After all their hard work, owners often end up in a place far from the one they envisioned.

Unfortunately, too often owners blow the money, lose it, handle their transition badly, or create feuding among their relatives. After all their hard work, owners often end in a place very far from the one they envisioned. It is vital that owners envision their post-business life long before the sale is final. Helpful questions include, "How much money or income do I need to maintain my lifestyle after the sale?" "Should I take a much-desired vacation?" "What will I do with my time after the sale or transition?" For most small business owners, the business makes up 70-90 percent of their net worth. When the business finally sells, it creates a massive liquidity event for which many are not prepared.

It generally requires a different skill set to manage a $30 million company than it does to manage a $30 million pool of capital. Don't presume that because you could run the company well, you can also run the capital well. Once a sale goes through, owners should eventually take measures to diversify their holdings in order to lower risk. The best way to address redeployment of assets is through a comprehensive wealth management plan that determines how much income is needed to keep pace with inflation and provides the owner with the lifestyle he desires.

You should be patient at this stage of the game. Any decisions made quickly will likely be bad decisions. Take your time and be careful of those who may want to take advantage of your new wealth. Though you will be very proud of yourself for having sold your business for real money, it is best that you keep it a secret to all but those it is absolutely necessary to share it with. Wealth is a burden as well as a blessing to you and your family.

An old rule of thumb is that an owner may draw down up to 4 percent annually from a balanced portfolio with a reasonably high expectation of not running out of money during his lifetime. However, in today's volatile conditions it is important for owners and their wealth managers to stay on their toes and review their plan frequently. The world presents a variety of options for spending your time. You can start a new business, spend time with the family, travel, or give your time and resources to charity. These are all worthwhile post-exit endeavors, but I cannot tell you where to spend your time; that is something you must wrestle through on your own. What to do after your exit is a tough question that deserves careful consideration and thought.

I recommend you read a book entitled Halftime by Bob Buford. The ultimate question of the book is: What do you do after you have found success? Where do you go from there? In essence, the book was written to help people navigate the treacherous waters of a midlife crisis, but I think it applies very much to the post-exit business owner who is looking for a new endeavor in which he can invest his time.

Bob Buford was a successful cable television executive who had it all together. He was massively successful in the business world. He had more money than he knew what to do with, and he had a wife and son that were the pride and joy of his life. By all accounts he had made it, but he still felt like something was missing, something of *significance*. When his son died in a tragic swimming accident, Buford was forced to re-evaluate his priorities. What he found changed the course of his life forever.

Buford divides a person's career into three main phases: first half, halftime, and the second half. Rather than see a worker's golden years as a time of decline, Buford looks at the second half of a person's career as a time to start something new, to *begin again*. According to Buford, the first half is all about success. Most first-halfers are charging ahead, looking for the next big deal, job, or project in order to maximize their bank accounts and status. But after a while, all that chasing starts to wear them down.[xl]

In our context, the first half would be building your business. This is the part of life that most, if not all of you, have already been through. I'm sure you do not need me to remind you of the time you spent eating Ramen noodles, moving to a new city, wondering if your business was going to make it, and questioning how you were going to pay your employees. Maybe the start of your business was smoother than that, but I know that every business owner has rough patches where he wonders how he will continue.

I also don't have to remind you what the growth years were like. The times when you had big deals on the table, when revenue was spiking, when you had so much growth you didn't know what to do with it. Those were the years when you were married to the game, when you worked long and hard and read everything you could get your hands on that would help you be the best.

These years, from the humble beginnings to the moment you realized that you had, in fact arrived, are all part of the first half. When you are enjoying success it is very, very easy to become overconfident and to feel that you are invincible. Pride is the most dangerous mindset you can have, and it will get you into a world of trouble. I know that my own pride led me into mistakes I wish I had never made.

Sometimes the first half of your career lasts twenty to thirty years; sometimes it is considerably shorter. Either way, you will know when it happens to you. Before you can recognize what is happening, it hits you; landing the big client, or paycheck, or sale doesn't taste quite as sweet. Your life accomplishments in the first half have started to fade in significance. What will you do in this moment of indecision? According to Buford, what you decide to do at halftime will determine the outcome of your second half.

Halftime is the perfect time to take a step back.

Halftime is the perfect time to take a step back. Call a timeout. Re-evaluate your life and impact. Instead of buying a new car or relocating to a new place, search for opportunities to use your expertise to build something in the second half—something of significance that will outlast you. What you do after you exit your business will impact your legacy far more than how much cash you leave.

Remember that even though I have focused very much on your eventual transition, going through the process does not mean you have to pull the trigger right away. It doesn't even necessarily mean you have to immediately step back either. What it does is give you the peace of mind to know that you can. It helps you rest easy at night knowing you have a plan in place should something go wrong. The BraveHeart Plan helps you build a management team and assemble a team of advisors who are watching your back. Even if you do not ever fully leave your business until your death, the BraveHeart Process is well worth the effort. It is not just an exit plan; it is an all-encompassing process that integrates family, business growth, exit planning, and wealth management.

You sit every day at the hub, at the nexus, of all of these decisions that are extremely complex and have far-reaching consequences. It is my true concern that you may not know what you do not know. If you are reading this book, I have no doubt that you are unparalleled in your field, but that does not mean you are equipped to deal with all of the issues that you are facing. Frankly, no one is. No one person has all the tools to deal with tax, law, investing, accounting, family issues, business growth and much more. You need a team. You need someone to pull it all together with you.

You need someone to pull it all together with you.

The BraveHeart Process gives you the concrete framework to live your best half-time life, helping to re-evaluate your priorities and start in a new direction. It is the philosophical and internal process of transitioning out of your traditional mindset. It opens the door for honest internal and external conversation: What do you want to do with your life after you leave? Do you want to stay on in a limited capacity? Do you want to cash out and move on? If you are going to move on, what will you do with your free time?

Transitioning from a business opens up a world of opportunity. You can devote your time to philanthropy, community volunteering, and church events. I love to help clients with their charitable giving endeavors. That is the fun stuff. You could set up a charitable foundation, a donor-advised fund, or whatever structure fits your family needs.

One of our team members, Herb McCarthy, was vice president with Billy Graham Evangelistic Association. He has helped create and advise hundreds of charities. As you enter the charitable world in a bigger way than just locally, it is wise to have someone with experience investigate the charities you are considering, to make sure they use the money wisely. There is a lot of fraud in the charitable world. One of the biggest advantages of the BraveHeart Planning Process™ is that it can give you a great amount of freedom.

> One of the biggest advantages of the BraveHeart Planning Process is that it can give you freedom.

Too many owners are tied down to their business, feeling like it cannot operate without them. While this is a gratifying notion to have, it is incredibly draining. If you have to be at the business all the time, in every meeting, on every phone call, looking over everyone's shoulder, it will suck all of the energy and time out of your life. I am not saying you should throw everything to the wind and hold no one accountable. You need to have controls in place because people are people and they will let you down. They will be selfish. One of my favorite quotes is from President Ronald Reagan: "Trust, but verify!"[xli] That being said, having a team that operates in your absence can give you freedom to travel, to take that vacation you've always wanted to go on but never had the time and to invest your life in things other than your business.

My brother David has done a very nice job internalizing this principle. He has the ability to travel when he chooses because he has trained a COO for twenty years on running his company. He makes sure that every manager has a suitable replacement. He created a system of checks and balances so that one person isn't handling the money. Everyone has accountability. He still is involved, making sure all the big decisions go through him, but the day-to-day operations of the business run smoothly without him. He focuses his time working on the business, not in it.

Another worthy post-exit activity is mentoring young people. As a business owner you are uniquely positioned to help struggling young people start their careers. Today's job market is not what it used to be, and young professionals need all the help they can get. My son's alma mater, University of North Carolina at Wilmington, has a unique program called the Cameron Executive Network that pairs retired executives with college juniors. Most of them meet once a week to discuss career-related topics of interest to the student. The program is a smashing success. The students love the advice and friendship from a more experienced businessperson, and the executives love the chance to get involved by giving back to the community.

If mentoring is not for you, or not enough to keep you busy, you could also start a new business or join an advisory group. Just because you exit doesn't mean you have to retire. If you still love what you do, if you love being a part of the action, if you still love the game, don't just quit. The worst thing you can do after your exit is sit on a pile of cash and be bored out of your mind.

I have seen too many owners sell out and then throw around cash like they are big shot investors. They start buying up lots of real estate and investing in startup firms. Being successful in your business does not necessarily give you an advantage in unrelated businesses. Building a business and investing in others are two different skills.

> **Transitioning from success to significance doesn't happen by itself; it takes a team dedicated to the win and a coach who knows how to get there.**

With a substantial part of your cash, you should work with a wealth manager who knows how to diversify across asset classes. If you still want to invest in private equity or venture capital, set aside some fun money, but don't put in any money you can't afford to lose. In my experience, investing outside your area of expertise is a bad idea. The investors on *Shark Tank* say the same: Never invest in something you do not understand.

Too many incredibly successful business leaders are stuck at the end of their sale, wondering what to do next with their talents. Maybe it's time to for you to realize that it is halftime for you and that you need to evaluate what truly matters to you. How do you want your second half to look? Talk it out with your loved ones, strategize with your trusted advisors, and make a plan. Transitioning from success to significance doesn't happen by itself; it takes a team dedicated to the win and a coach who knows how to get there.

CHAPTER 12

It Takes a BraveHeart

Edinburgh, Scotland, November 1, 1292 A.D.

On a dark and stormy night in 1286, a freak accident sealed the fate of an entire kingdom. King Alexander III of Scotland presided over a golden age of peace and prosperity for Scotland. But he had no successor, no lion to step up and carry on his legacy. The king's three children had all preceded him in death, though the middle-aged king was no more than forty-four years old. His fortune, however, was about to change. The King had just gotten married, and the night was spent in celebration of his new bride's birthday at the castle of Edinburgh.

At the party's end, Alexander gathered up his entourage to ride off. His royal advisors begged him not to travel through the dark of night in dangerous weather, but the king wouldn't listen. He was as healthy as a bull and stubborn as a mule. Mounting up on his great steed, Alexander galloped into the night, never to see the sun's rays again. Somewhere along the way, the king was separated from his companions by the storm's fury. Alone, his horse lost its footing and plunged over the edge of an embankment. The king was found dead, washed up on the shores of the sea the next morning.

Upon the death of the king, the crown was passed to his three-year-old granddaughter, Margaret, the Maid of Norway. After Alexander's death, the Guardians of Scotland, or Margaret's ruling regents as they were known, signed a treaty with the English that provided for Margaret's eventual marriage to the heir-apparent of the English Crown, Edward Caernarvon. When the young queen died on her journey to Scotland, the Guardians invited Edward

I of England to arbitrate between the competing claims to the throne, namely John Balliol, Lord of Galloway, and Robert the Bruce.

The Guardians were trying to prevent bloodshed between the contending parties, but instead they brought open war upon themselves. Bringing in Edward was like inviting a lion to a wolf hunt. The lion may stop the infighting over scraps, but he also takes the lion's share for himself. Edward saw the situation as an opportunity to be exploited. He demanded that his claim to the feudal overlordship of Scotland be recognized or he wouldn't lift a finger to help. The Scottish nobles grudgingly agreed, though as individuals, not as a nation. Their greed for the throne and fear over losing their lands in England blinded them to Edward's nefarious designs.

In November of 1292, a great feudal court set up by Edward bestowed the crown on John Balliol. Losing no time, Edward designated his own son as Balliol's heir. Eventually Balliol renounced his homage to the English throne and so Edward invaded Scotland, sacking border towns and defeating the Scots at the Battle of Dunbar. By July, Edward had forced Balliol to renounce the throne.

With the country in chaos and the aristocracy in full retreat, Edward might have been successful in his bid for Scottish submission, if it had not been for the valiance of William Wallace. After his assassination of the Sheriff William de Heselrig and the bold raid on the city of Scone, resistance fighters flocked to Wallace's side. Wallace pressed his advantage, and four months later took his stand at the Battle of Sterling Bridge against a professional English Army of thirteen thousand trained soldiers.

Though vastly outnumbered, Wallace caught the English by surprise as they were crossing the river over the narrow Sterling Bridge. Wallace waited to attack until half the army had passed. When the time was right, he sent in his phalanx of spearmen followed by heavy cavalry. A crucial charge by Wallace's lieutenant broke the English ranks, pushing them back into the river. The bridge collapsed under the weight of retreating English soldiers. The men fortunate enough to escape Wallace's blade met a similar fate in a watery grave.

After the battle, Wallace took on the mantle of Guardian of Scotland on behalf of John Balliol, true king of Scotland. Wallace reigned until his defeat at Falkirk and subsequent betrayal and capture by the English. King Edward had Wallace shipped to London to stand trial as a traitor to the crown. When they read his crimes before the court, Wallace had only this to say: "I cannot be a traitor to Edward, for I was never his subject."

William Wallace was sentenced to be tortured and executed, his only crime defending the country he loved so dearly. He was dragged through London, drawn and quartered, and then beheaded. His death ended his life, but not his legacy. Inspired by his courage, Robert the Bruce took up Wallace's mantle, eventually defeating the English and reclaiming the Scottish Crown.

My heart stirs every time I read his story. The story of William and those who fought with him inspires me. It is not because they were such extraordinary fighters or legendary warriors, but precisely because they were the opposite. They were commoners. Wallace's men were mostly peasant farmers and blacksmiths, merchants and laborers. They had no horses or titles, no lands or dominions. They didn't fight for gold, or thrones, or kings, or glory. They fought for freedom.

War is brutal, ugly, and savage, but it has shaped human destiny since the dawn of time. It forces people to desperation and pushes them beyond their limits. It brings out the worst in people, but it also reveals what is best. In the midst of incredibly dark times, solitary torches sometimes flame to light the way. Wallace was one of those torches.

Many of the patriots that fought in Revolutionary War descended from those humble Scottish Independence fighters. Like their forefathers, the Revolutionaries rose up against the oppression of the British government. The Continental Army, kin to those Scottish freedom fighters, was composed of ordinary men. They were carpenters and sailors, farmers and tailors. Paul Revere was a silversmith, George Washington was a farmer, and John Hancock was a merchant. They were no barons of England, they had no titles of nobility, and they fought for no material gain. Our Founding Fathers fought for freedom.

The battleground for freedom stretches far and wide. It stretches beyond the fields of war, for it is not merely threatened by foreign despots and enemy combatants. We all must fight for freedom, whether we are soldiers or businessmen. As Ronald Reagan once said, "Freedom is never more than one generation away from extinction. We didn't pass it on to our children in the bloodstream. It must be fought for, protected, and handed on for them to do the same, or one day we will spend our sunset years telling our children and our children's children what it was once like in the United States where men were free." Even now, our religious freedom is being sacrificed on the altar of political correctness. When I look back over my life, the number of individual freedoms we have lost since I was young is absolutely terrifying. The bondage of big government continues to grow through more laws, more regulations and ever higher taxation. According to the Heritage Foundation, the US is ranked only number 12 in the 2015 Index of Economic Freedom, under its "Mostly Free" category. Our score is 76.2 out of a possible 100.

Not only are there external threats, but also internal. There are all sorts of bondages in life, from addictions to financial implosion. We can overcome them, but we must first find our courage. Courage reposes in the hearts of warriors on the battlefield, but it also rests in the hearts of the everyday men and women who choose to run their businesses in the face of continued challenges. Courage finds its place in the hard choices of ordinary life. Courage is the defining quality of a BraveHeart. I use war as an analogy because business can often feel like war. It is a constant competition, a constant fight. Many owners feel like they are trapped in an uphill battle, with the advantage all to the enemy. I wrote this book because I hate to see owners trapped in bondage to debt, chained to their desk, or weighed down with obligation and stress. I started the business I work in now because I care deeply about freedom. In fact, I have dedicated my career to helping business owners achieve the freedom for which they have worked so hard.

As we saw with Alexander the Great and Richard the Lionheart, it is not enough just to fight. It makes no difference if you win or lose if you are fighting for the wrong objective. Freedom without virtue is anarchy. I have worked with hundreds of business owners over my career, but rarely with the selfish ones. Owners that are in the game because they love the prestige, or being "the man," or having a high profile never last long as my client. I don't work with clients that measure their self-worth in commas and zeros. The true BraveHearts of the business world fight for freedom and they fight for their families. They do what is hard because it is right. It is not easy to own your own business and to work with your family. As I pointed out in the introduction, most family businesses do not make it past the first generation; a few make it past the second; and only a tiny minority make it to the third and beyond. It's not easy to be successful in family business, but BraveHearts work at it every day.

> I don't want you to be merely successful; I want you to live and leave a legacy.

If you have made it to the place where you can lay your head down at night and not wonder if the business will be there in six months, you have accomplished something incredible. If you have the time and energy to step back and work on your business instead of in it, you have made it further than 95 percent of owners. I do not want to take away from what you have already accomplished, but as a fellow business owner, I know that you cannot stay where you are. In business, as well as in life, if you are not moving forward, you are moving backwards. Anything that isn't growing is dying, or already dead. I don't want you to be merely successful; I want you to live and leave a legacy. I want your life to have significance.

I have loved working with families over generations. I can see that people really do reap what they sow, often in the lives of their children and grandchildren. The parents that ignore their children, coddle them, or neglect to teach them, often end up with broken families. Their children self-destruct, starting a cycle that sometimes lasts for generations. The parents that teach their children well in every area of life, tend to have families that love each other, work hard, and share common values. These Legacy Families sometimes last for generations, living lives of significance that they learned from their ancestors.

The Larkspur family is one of these Legacy Families. Though the family has suffered numerous tragedies, I see the gift of love evidenced in their lives. I was brought in to do estate planning for what I will refer to as the first generation back in the early 1990s. They were in their late 80s. They were delightful people. Next, the family asked me to handle the estate for a grandson (third generation), who had died leaving a wife and children. The family had not planned for that contingency. However, they learned from that situation. They now include the younger generations in every area of their farming business and have them do their own estate planning for their own families. People do not always die in the order you expect, which is why planning is so vital.

After settling the grandson's estate, the Larkspurs experienced another unexpected death. The second generation owner passed away only a few short years after his son. Though his early death was a great loss to the family, we were prepared, having planned his estate and business transition. Because of that wise planning and the love the family shows for each other, the third generation surviving sons have remained good friends for these past twenty years since their dad's death, the Larkspur legacy lives on well—financially and relationally.

We recently included the fourth generation children in the business and estate planning. They have worked in the business for some years now and also have their own children that we need to protect and prepare for their business opportunities when they come of age. The fourth generation work well together and love each other, continuing the practices that I saw started by the wonderful legacy of family and business created by the first generation. It is the American dream, and they are living it.

The Larkspurs are not a perfect family. They have their share of challenges, just like any family. All families face tough times. All of us have had difficult situations in our past. Our parents and grandparents passed on to us their own hurts and deficiencies and we have added our own. But we cannot use that as an excuse to keep us from doing what is right from now on. I have set forth our 7-step BraveHeart Planning Process™ in this book to enable you to grow a business, prepare it for sale or transition and to build in protections for your business and family along the way, should unforeseen circumstances arise. Now that you have a guidebook, you can create your own particular roadmap from it. Remember, a good exit takes time. Consider that the process will take years, not months. The earlier you start preparing, the more likely your exit will be a happy and successful one for you and your family.

Developing your own BraveHeart Plan is something you *can* do. It will not be easy, and you will have to make tough decisions. But it is both your privilege and your duty. If you plan to sell your business, it will only be more difficult in the years to come. If you transition to the next generation, you have a different set of challenges. In either scenario, you can create a legacy of faith in God, family and financial security that can last for many generations.

It takes guts. It takes determination but together we can recapture the spirit of entrepreneurism and hope in the future. Let us take up the fight to make this world a better place to live in for our children and our grandchildren by building families and businesses that thrive and endure for generations. It isn't easy but don't let anyone convince you that it is impossible! Too often people give up right before the finish line

Remember, to be a BraveHeart is not for the faint of heart. It is a code; it is a process; and it is a movement. Those who ascribe to the creed are not born, they are built. They follow through and finish. They fight for family and freedom. They build legacies.

Begin today.

Live it brave!

Reminders to Owners

An exit process can take years to develop and execute, which is why it is so important to start as soon as you can. Transitioning is the most crucial phase of your career. It is complex, complicated, and requires a delicate touch. There is a lot that goes into planning your exit. There is no doubt that you will exit the business. The question is whether you will exit well. The more prepared you are, the better for everyone.

You need to be clear about who you are, what you want out of the sale or transition and why you are deciding to plan your exit. Also be clear about the buyer you choose or to whom you are transitioning. You need to understand what it is they want and why they want it. Knowing all of that could prevent you from making serious mistakes as you settle on a buyer or successor. Please spend adequate time understanding the "who's" and "why's"—before you start engaging any third parties toward a sale or succession.

Because you must begin your journey well in order to end it well, choose your BraveHeart Planning™ team wisely. The team you assemble will need to examine most areas of your life. You'll want those best suited to your situation.

If you are an owner that cares deeply about your employees, you will need to be very cautious about the proposed buyer. If you want your culture and employees protected, it may be best to sell to a buyer who requires your management team to stay intact.

Keep in mind as you plan for the transition or sale of your company, you need to plan to be going to something, so you are not lost when the transition closes. Understand that generally entrepreneurs do not do well in retirement and they often make bad employees, so plan accordingly.

Finally, know that managing money is a different skill set than managing a company; be very careful about how you invest upon sale. Too many invest quickly and aggressively. It is almost always a mistake. You are not likely to have much experience with it, so take plenty of time to redeploy the capital. On this point, it is wise to seek wisdom in a multitude of counselors, including others that have sold businesses.

(ENDNOTES)

1 Webb, James H. *Born Fighting: How the Scots-Irish Shaped America*. New York: Broadway, 2004. Print.

2 *Astrachan, J.H. and Shanker, M.C. (2003), Family Businesses' Contribution to the U.S. Economy: A Closer Look. (http://coles. kennesaw.edu/centers/cox-family-enterprise/cox-family-documents/ FB-in-US-2003.pdf).*

3 *Clifton, Jim. "American Entrepreneurship: Dead or Alive?" American Entrepreneurship: Dead or Alive? Gallup, 13 Jan. 2015. Web. 05 May 2015. <http://www.gallup.com/businessjournal/180431/american-entrepreneurship-dead-alive.aspx>.*

4 Ibn-Ḥaldūn, 'Abd-ar-Raḥmān Ibn-Muḥammad. "Chapter 3." *The Muqaddimah*. Princeton, NJ: Princeton U, 1967. N. pag. Print.

5 *Zellweger, Nason, Nordqvist. From Longevity of Firms to Transgenerational Entrepreneurship of Families: Introducing Family Entrepreneurial Orientation. Retrieved November 2012: (http://c. ymcdn.com/sites/www.ffi.org/resource/resmgr/docs/goodman_study.pdf.)*

6 *Mass Mutual Family Business Survey*

7 *Dorman, Mark. "Building a Successful Transition Plan" Dorman Legacy Advisors, (http://MidwestFamilyBusinessCenter.com)*

8 *Family Business Alliance. Retrieved June 2014:(http://www.fbagr.org/ index.php?option=com_content&view=article&id=117&Itemid=75*

9 TNS Global, Phoenix Wealth Survey and PricewaterhouseCoopers.

10 *Mass Mutual Family Business Survey, 2007*

11   *John Brown. "Exit Planning Work Book." 2011. Business Enterprise Institute*

12   *Ruffenach, Glenn. "The Retirement Lies We Tell Ourselves." WSJ. Wall Street Journal, 1 Dec. 2006. Web. 01 July 2015. <http://www. wsj.com/articles/SB116544325824442699>.*

13   *Ruth Helman, Mathew Greenwald and Associates, Craig Copeland, and Jack Vanderhei. December 11ᵗʰ, 2006 page R-4. "Will More of Us Be Working Forever?" The 2006 Retirement Confidence Survey, Issue Brief No. 292, April 2006.*

14   Mullaney, William J. "Department of Labor and the Department of the Treasury RFI Regarding Lifetime Income Options for Participants and Beneficiaries in Retirement Plans", page 41 (Filed electronically on May 3, 2010). MetLife. Web.

15   *"Whose Business Is It Anyway? Smart Strategies For Ownership Succession," PricewaterhouseCoopers*

16   *Aronoff, Craig E., Stephen L. McClure, and John L. Ward. "The Pieces of the Succession Puzzle." Family Business Succession: The Final Test of Greatness. New York: Palgrave Macmillan, 2011. 13-14. Print.*

17   PWC Family Business Survey, 2012/2013

18   *Brown, John H., Kevin M. Short, and Kathryn B. Carroll. "Get Top Dollar--And More--Selling Your Business." Cash out Move On: Get Top Dollar, and More, Selling Your Business. Golden, CO: Business Enterprise Institute, 2008. 108-09. Print.*

19   *Patrick M. Foley, Exit: Should You Sell Your Business? How? And Then What? Robert W. Baird and Co.*

20   Bowen, John, CEG Worldwide

21   *Mercer, Chris. The 1% Solution for Managing Pre-Liquid Wealth. Memphis: Mercer Capital, n.d. Print.*

22   *"Is Your Business Worth What You Think It Is?" Deloitte & Touche LLP – Canada, 2006*

23 *Cope, Paula. Cope and Associates.* Brown, J. & Short, K. *Cash Out Move On- Get Top Dollar and More Selling Your Business.* Business Enterprise Press, 2008.

24 *Brown, John H., Kevin M. Short, and Kathryn B. Carroll. "Get Top Dollar--And More--Selling Your Business." Cash out Move On: Get Top Dollar, and More, Selling Your Business. Golden, CO: Business Enterprise Institute, 2008. 108-09. Print.*

25 *Family Business Alliance. Retrieved June 2014:(http://www.fbagr.org/ index.php?option=com_content&view=article&id=117&Itemid=75)*

26 Taibbi, Matt. "Ripping Off Young America: The College-Loan Scandal." *Rolling Stone.* Rolling Stone, 15 Aug. 2013. Web. 06 May 2015. <http://www.rollingstone.com/politics/news/ripping-off-young-america-the-college-loan-scandal-20130815>

27 Tomin, Carolynn, and Colleen Carcone. "Gifts to Minors." *Principles of Estate Planning.* Kentucky: National Underwriter, 2012. 197-98. Print.

28 "2014 Donor-Advised-Fund Report." *NPTrust.org.* National Philanthropic Trust, n.d. Web. 06 May 2015. <http://www.nptrust. org/daf-report/>.

29 Marshall, Eric. "Set Up Your Dynasty Trust" *The Family Office Blue Print.*

30 Aristotle. "Poetics." Trans. Ingram Bywater. The Project Gutenberg EBook. Oxford: Clarendon P, 2 May 2009. Web. 26 Oct. 2014.

31 "Since 1526." *World of Beretta.* Beretta, n.d. Web. <http://www. beretta.com/en-us/world-of-beretta/since-1526/>.

32 Dalton, Michael A., Joseph M. Gillice, James F. Dalton, Thomas P. Langdon, and Michael A. Dalton. *Insurance Planning.* Third ed. Los Angeles: Money Education, 2013. Print.

33 Dalton, Michael A., Joseph M. Gillice, James F. Dalton, Thomas P. Langdon, and Michael A. Dalton. *Insurance Planning.* Third ed. Los Angeles: Money Education, 2013. Print.

34 Preisser, Vic. *Family Meetings*. Pasadena: Institute for Preparing Heirs, 2014. Print.

35 Prince. Russ, Alan and Brett Van Bortel. *Rainmaker*. Cincinnati: The National Underwriter Company. 2006. Print.

36 Runciman, Steven. *A History of the Crusades: Volume 3: The Kingdom of Acre and the Later Crusades*. Harmondsworth: Penguin, 1965. Print.

37 *Aronoff, Craig E., Stephen L. McClure, and John L. Ward. "The Pieces of the Succession Puzzle." Family Business Succession: The Final Test of Greatness. New York: Palgrave Macmillan, 2011 Print.*

38 DeSanty, Tina M. "Sec. 1202: Small Business Stock Capital Gains Exclusion ." *Sec. 1202: Small Business Stock Capital Gains Exclusion*. American Institute of CPAs, 1 May 2013. Web. 09 July 2015. http://www.aicpa.org/publications/taxadviser/2013/may/pages/clinic_may2013-story-07.aspx.

39 Porter, Michael E. *Competitive Advantage: Creating and Sustaining Superior Performance*. New York: Free, 1985. Print.

40 Buford, Bob. *Halftime: Changing Your Game Plan from Success to Significance*. Grand Rapids, MI: Zondervan, 1994. Print.

41 Ronald Reagan Quote." *BrainyQuote*. Xplore, n.d. Web. 06 May 2015. <http://www.brainyquote.com/quotes/quotes/r/ronaldreag147717.html>.

ABOUT THE AUTHOR

Randy M. Long, JD, CFP®, CExP™, is the Founder/CEO of Long Business Advisors, LLC, a consulting firm that specializes in building, transitioning, and managing the sale of BraveHeart businesses. Randy is President of Long Family Office, Inc., a firm serving high net-worth families. He is also the creator of *The BraveHeart Planning Process*™, which is designed to help you, the business owner, prepare to sell or transition your business to whomever you choose, whenever you desire, for the amount you need to be financially independent.

Randy has spent over thirty years planning, advising and consulting family businesses. He uses his background as an estate planning and business lawyer, wealth manager, and exit planner to help you build a roadmap that is right for you, your family, and your employees.